THE
CREATIVE
ENTREPRENEUR

THE
CREATIVE
ENTREPRENEUR

Isa Maria Seminega

ilex

THE CREATIVE ENTREPRENEUR

An Hachette UK Company
www.hachette.co.uk
First published in Great Britain in 2015 by
ILEX, a division of Octopus Publishing Group Ltd

Octopus Publishing Group
Carmelite House
50 Victoria Embankment
London, EC4Y 0DZ
www.octopusbooks.co.uk

Publisher: Roly Allen
Commissioning Editor: Zara Larcombe
Senior Project Editor: Natalia Price-Cabrera
Managing Specialist Editor: Frank Gallaugher
Editor: Rachel Silverlight
Art Director: Julie Weir
Designer: Anders Hanson
Production Controller: Sarah-Jayne Johnson

ISBN 978-1-78157-270-2

A CIP catalogue record for this book is
available from the British Library

Printed and bound in China

10 9 8 7 6 5 4 3 2 1

THE
CREATIVE
BUSINESS

Taking a leap to start your own business is risky. Everyone will make a point of telling you so. What they won't tell you is that working for someone else can be just as risky. The jobs market is becoming harder and harder to navigate, with people who have been in secure jobs for years finding themselves thrown on the scrap heap at the first hint of trouble.

I should know, I was one of them. I was made redundant at the height of the recession and all at once the job security I'd been promised was nothing but hollow words.

Instead of trusting my future to another company, I decided to take charge of my own life and start a business doing something I loved (and hopefully make more money in the process). Since then I've been on a mission to help creative entrepreneurs build profitable businesses on their terms.

Now, I want to help you do the same.

Every year, hundreds of thousands of people talk about starting a new business, but most of them never take that first step to get their ideas off the ground. They make excuses like "I'm waiting for the right time" or "I don't have enough money." But that's just it, they are excuses. There will never be the right time to start a business and you will never have enough money. You just have to decide what it is you really want and find a way to make it happen.

It's relatively easy to become a creative entrepreneur: all you really need is internet access, something to offer, and a way of getting paid. It's a lot harder to stand out from the crowd and build a long-lasting, sustainable business. It can be done, of course, but many entrepreneurs won't last the distance because of the hard and often stressful work involved.

At the start-up stages, the amount of information you encounter can be overwhelming. Then, when you finally feel that you are getting the hang of things, you'll encounter new challenges and problems that test your patience. Sales might stagnate, a competitor might copy your product range, or you might need to radically change your marketing techniques.

However, starting a business also means the freedom to create the life of your dreams. You can keep your business intentionally small, or you can grow it into a global brand.

Whatever your goals, this book will help you get there. Think of it as your own personal business guide—a roadmap for starting a creative business and for growing it into a thriving, profitable empire. You can work through the book chapter by chapter and use it to build your own unique strategy, or you can dip in and out when you have a question, or a new challenge comes your way.

1

LAY THE
GROUNDWORK

BUSINESS MODELS, SIMPLIFIED

At a most basic level, a business model is how the business intends to make money. It's a framework for creating economic value and, let's face it, without profit, there is no business, so it is imperative you get this part right.

A business model consists of nine basic building blocks that work together to form your business blueprint.

Seeing how these elements work and fit together can help you spot opportunities for innovation or to differentiate your business from the competition. Your business model isn't set in stone; in fact, reassessing it on an annual basis is advised, so you can evolve and adapt to market changes.

Putting your business model together is like piecing together a puzzle. The easiest way to set things out and see how they work together is to use the business model canvas framework.

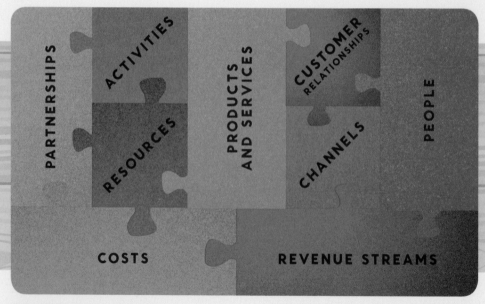

BUSINESS MODEL CANVAS
The nine building blocks of business model design.

CORE ELEMENTS OF A BUSINESS MODEL

1. PRODUCTS AND SERVICES

What do you sell? Think about all the options available to your customers. This could be products, services, or both. Which problems are you helping to solve or which need does your business satisfy?

2. PEOPLE

Who are you selling to? Who are you solving a problem or need for? Segment the customers. Does what you are selling match their needs?

3. CHANNELS

Channels are customer touch points that help you build your customer experience. How are you reaching and communicating with your people to deliver your product or service? Will you be selling direct through a website, via a retail outlet, in person, or through door-to-door sales? Which channels work best?

4. CUSTOMER RELATIONSHIPS

How are you building and maintaining relationships? What type of relationship do each of your customer segments expect you to establish and maintain with them? Social media, blogging, email, and networking events are all examples of ways you can connect and stay in touch with your customers.

5. REVENUE STREAMS

What is the revenue model? What pricing strategies are you using? Consider subscriptions fees, licensing models, and fixed pricing. What works best? How do your customers want to pay?

6. RESOURCES

What are the most important things you need to make your business work? Consider the financial, physical, intellectual or human resources you may need. Start-up money for equipment? A physical space to sell from? Additional training or qualifications? Employees?

7. ACTIVITIES

These are what you need to do to keep your business running, communicate with customers, and deliver value. Don't just consider the administrative tasks; also think about how you will keep your business thriving. It might include developing new products and services or coming up with new ideas.

8. PARTNERSHIPS

Who are your key business partners, sponsors, retailers, and collaborators?

9. COSTS

This is how much money is needed to run your business, make your products, and find new customers. Ask yourself what the most expensive resources and activities are that you need to undertake?

HOW TO DECIDE ON A BUSINESS IDEA

There are two main ways to find a business idea: either you look for one, or one finds you.
The first method involves looking for a gap in the market and actively searching for an idea that you think has the best chance of making you money. The second involves an idea that presents itself to you—you might decide to turn something you love into a business, or notice an opportunity that you simply can't ignore.

Most creative entrepreneurs have lots of different interests and passions, which can lead to multiple business ideas. This is better than not having any ideas at all, but it can make it very difficult to choose the right one to move forward with.

HOW DO YOU DECIDE WHICH IDEA IS BEST FOR YOU?

ARE YOU PASSIONATE ABOUT IT?
You don't have to combine all of your interests when creating your business model—in fact, it is actually better to keep some things as a hobby. Just because you enjoy something doesn't mean you need to make it into a business or do it professionally, even if you're great at it.

But you do need some passion for what you do. After all, you will be doing it every day for the foreseeable future. Ask yourself, can you see yourself doing this for 30–40 hours a week for the next few years? If your answer's "yes," then that's a great starting point.

WHICH IDEA DO YOU FEEL MOST PASSIONATE ABOUT?
It is best to start off with one main idea or passion, as juggling too many at once can lead to exhaustion. Running just one business is hard enough, but complicating it with more than one main idea can lead to you having to split your time between them. Consequently, neither will have your full focus, which will make it harder to get the results you're looking for. So, start with one main business idea—you can always add more later.

WHICH HAS THE BEST POTENTIAL FOR MAKING MONEY?
Instead of worrying whether an idea is good or not, determine whether it is something your potential target market is looking for.

If all of your ideas have potential, then look at what your target market might want to buy from you. They not only need to be able to afford what you are offering, but they also have to *want* to buy it from you.

OTHER THINGS TO CONSIDER

STUDY LONG-TERM TRENDS

What external factors might impact your business in the future? Will people still have a need for your product in a few years' time? How is society changing? Where is your industry headed? Think about the opportunities and challenges that could come your way. Is it worth it? Will you still want to run a business using this idea, despite the many issues you might face?

LOOK AT THE PURPOSE OF THE PRODUCT OR SERVICE

Is your product or service something that people want? If there is a valid reason why people will want what you intend to make, then do it. Maybe your product is also functional and fulfills an important need, or maybe your services will help others learn something new or become a better version of themselves.

STUDY THE COMPETITION

This can help you to see if your unique talents are a good fit for customers. Even if there are other companies selling similar products and services, you may be able to differentiate yourself or serve an alternate niche. Sometimes there is still an overlap, but if it's clear how you can do things differently then you can still evolve the idea into a profitable business.

TEST YOUR IDEA

Validate your idea by talking with actual potential customers. You can do this in person at networking events or focus groups, or you can set up a simple website and landing page to capture email addresses. Contact some of the people through email to discuss your idea and find out what motivated them to sign up. This will help you better understand why they are interested in your business. You can also test products out on family and friends by sharing samples and asking for constructive feedback.

DON'T LET FEAR STAND IN YOUR WAY AND PREVENT YOU FROM STARTING YOUR BUSINESS

The key thing at this stage is to pick an idea and get started. Even if things don't go to plan, you can refine and improve your idea, pivot, or move on.

ETINCELLE CREATIVE STUDIO

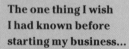

WHO: Marie Maglaque
WHAT: Fashion and jewelry design
WEBSITE: www.etincellecreativestudio.com

Before starting my business, I was afraid of...
I wasn't afraid of many things really, as my business grew organically. However, I am still not very sure about the business planning and finances parts. Figuring out my prices and fees was also a struggle—and still is!

The one thing I wish I had known before starting my business...
- Business planning
- Accounting
- Graphic design
- Coding (for websites)

My best tip for new creative business owners...
Be flexible and open-minded. If you work from home, make sure you regularly connect with like-minded people via networking events, attending exhibitions, and so on. From experience, new projects have often landed on my desk thanks to connections I have made over the past months, or even years.

My favorite thing about running my own business...
The flexibility and freedom that is offers. To me, this is priceless!

GIDDY KIPPER

WHO: Heidi Bowman (co-founder)
WHAT: Handmade home accessories
WEBSITE: www.giddykipper.net

Before starting my business, I was afraid of...

Everything! Not being able to afford to live, being a failure, how it would all work... I think it's probably the same for a lot of small businesses. In our case, we started a business out of necessity, due to our personal circumstances and with almost nothing in the bank. It was probably the scariest thing we've ever done!

The one thing I wish I had known before starting my business...

Just how much hard work it would be without funds at the start. Somehow we managed to get through, but there were a lot of early starts and very late finishes and some fairly close calls financially! It's not always the easy option to start your own business—we've never worked so hard, but at least we know it's for us.

My best tip for new creative business owners...

Try and get some financial backing initially. In our situation, we were both in it together. We had no other income and had to work so hard to get anywhere. Without finances for advertising, branding, vehicles, and so on, it can seem like a never-ending struggle. However, if you use your initiative you will find that anything is possible! Contact as many people as you can for free features— remember, magazines have lots of pages to fill every month, so if you have something worth sharing, make sure they see it!

My favorite thing about running my own business...

Being in charge of what we do. All the decisions are made by us, and as it's our business we can take it in any direction, which is very exciting. We're incredibly proud of our achievements. We've been featured in most of the national (and some international) home magazines, bridal magazines, and newspapers; on a huge amount of blogs; won two wedding awards; and been nominated for customer service awards. We've also raised two little boys at the same time, which is no mean feat!

①

WHY PASSION IS NOT ALWAYS ENOUGH

Starting a passion-fueled business is seductive. If it's a choice between working for someone else doing something uninspiring, or starting your own business doing something you love, then most people are going to choose the latter—who doesn't want the freedom to be their own boss and make their own choices every day? The problem comes when you realize that no one is going to make you a millionaire just because you are passionate about what you do.

Being passionate about something isn't a guarantee that you will be able to turn it into a profitable business. That's why we have the term "starving artist"! Artists create because they have to. They love and are passionate about what they create, but it takes more than that to get enough people to part with their cash so that you can have a comfortable life and a thriving business. It makes sense to assume that you'd make more money when you enjoy what you do, rather than when you are uninspired by your job, but that's only the case if people want what you are selling. Many creative entrepreneurs get so excited when they start their business that they put their all into making their products or indulging in the part of the business they are passionate about, only to realize that they forgot to get other people on board with what they are doing.

CONNECT WHAT YOU LOVE WITH WHAT OTHER PEOPLE CARE ABOUT

When you start a business with your passion or something you love as the focal point, you often don't begin with a business mindset. You are thinking about the fact that you get to do what you love all day. It's exciting. But before you start rushing off to make lots of something no one is going to buy, you need

to consider how you can turn this into an actual business opportunity. This part is critical to success. In business, you are not making for *you*—you are making for your customer, so you need to find a way to make sure they can relate to your service or products. What can your business do for them?

USE PASSION AS YOUR START POINT

The key to growing a profitable, sustainable business is taking your passion and evolving it into something that other people want to spend their hard-earned money on. They need to want what you make; it can't all be about you.

For example, maybe you're passionate about making treats for your dog. Your friends have told you that "you should totally sell these," and you think they're right. You love making the treats, researching ingredients, coming up with new recipes, and watching your dog gobble them up. You get so enamored with the idea of creating your own dog treat company that you start planning everything you'll need. You buy ingredients and supplies in bulk, build a website, and start choosing colors for your packaging. Your passion is driving you. You're excited and keeping yourself busy with the many tasks you need to do to get your business up and running. The only

problem is you forget you need a reason for people to buy them from you.

People aren't going to buy your dog treats just because you love making them. They will buy them if you convince them that it is something they want or need for their own dog. The focus has to be on the customer. Do your research. What treats do their dogs normally eat? How much would they be willing to pay for them? How many treats do you need to sell each week, month, or year to make a decent living out of it?

Your passion is the fuel for your business— it motivates you to create, and inspires you in the tough moments. But it's not the *focus* of your business. Use your passion as a focal point to discover how you can best serve others and fulfill their wants and needs. In this way you will have a much better chance of building a profitable business and avoiding "starving artist syndrome."

FIND YOUR SWEET SPOT

The key to getting paid for work you love is finding that point between what you are passionate about, what you are best at, and what people will pay you to do. Creative people are often multi-passionate and multi-talented and it can be hard to narrow down which skills and ideas to move forward with. Finding your sweet spot can help you decide what to focus on to ensure you can make money.

Your sweet spot is the point where what you love to do, what you do well, and what people will pay you to do, collide.

★ YOUR SWEET SPOT

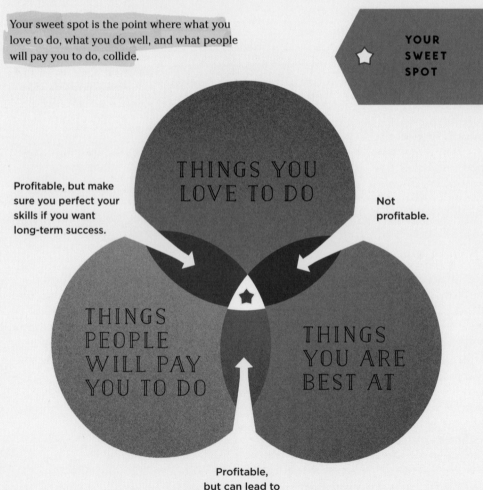

Profitable, but make sure you perfect your skills if you want long-term success.

THINGS YOU LOVE TO DO

Not profitable.

THINGS PEOPLE WILL PAY YOU TO DO

THINGS YOU ARE BEST AT

Profitable, but can lead to dissatisfaction and resentment.

WHAT IS YOUR SWEET SPOT?

Brainstorm each of the three categories. Be honest with yourself for the best results. Create and fill out your own circle diagram for the best answers, based on the one opposite. These questions are a useful starting point:

THINGS YOU LOVE TO DO

What are you most passionate about?

What do you feel happiest doing?

What do you have an insatiable need to keep learning about?

What do you believe in?

What do you want to be known for?

THINGS YOU ARE BEST AT

What do people always say you're good at?

What do they thank you for the most?

What can you teach people to do?

THINGS PEOPLE WILL PAY YOU TO DO

What have people said they would pay you to help with?

What services or products do customers always ask you for?

Send out a survey and ask your current customers what other services they would pay you for. What are the common answers?

Have you had any requests for specific services?

ANALYZING YOUR ANSWERS

THINGS YOU ARE REALLY GOOD AT AND PEOPLE WILL PAY YOU TO DO

If you are good at something that people will pay you for, but you don't like doing it, you could end up dissatisfied and eventually resenting your customers. Try brainstorming ways you can add in elements of things you love to differentiate your service and to ensure you enjoy the work longer term.

THINGS YOU LOVE TO DO AND PEOPLE WILL PAY YOU TO DO

If you love your work you will want to do it long term, and if people will pay you to do it then that's a bonus! To create a long-term sustainable business, though, you need to get really good at it. You want to become known for what you do and attract enough customers to ensure a long and happy work life. Solution: Keep learning, and hone those skills!

PURPOSE
AND VISION

WHAT IS THE PURPOSE OF YOUR BUSINESS?

The true purpose of your business is not just to make money. It should go deeper than that—all the way to what inspires you to do what you do. *That* is the reason why your business exists—making money is simply the result of what you do, not *why* you do it.

Your purpose is the driving force behind you getting up every day and is how you will make an impact in the world. Understanding your purpose is more than just a nice "to do" activity. In fact, if you want your business to make a difference, generate a decent living, and to make you feel happy and fulfilled while running it, then you need to know your "why"—the purpose behind what you do.

Purpose-driven businesses have a strong mission. This mission makes them different, helps guide different aspects of their business, and keeps them on track. Customers respond to businesses with an authentic and meaningful purpose behind

them. In fact, a 2014 study by Deloitte[1] discovered that businesses with a strong sense of purpose are more successful.

This makes sense. It's hard for customers to care about your business beyond what you can do for them, but if you are able to successfully articulate what you believe in and what you stand for, it creates an emotional connection that can be the start of a more meaningful relationship. Your customers will feel like they are contributing to something bigger, something important, and they are more likely to want to do business with you as a result.

THE BENEFITS OF HAVING A BUSINESS PURPOSE

DIFFERENTIATES YOUR BRAND AND BUSINESS

A strong purpose will help you stand out from similar businesses. Your purpose is unique to you, so it will create a different story and conversation to that of your competitors.

GIVES YOU SOMETHING TO STRIVE FOR AND THE MOTIVATION TO SUCCEED

Making more money can only motivate you to a certain point; your purpose gives you a reason to strive for something beyond money.It's your inspiration to achieve your best. Once your business starts making money, what will keep you working on it every day?

MAKES YOU MORE FOCUSED

When you have a deeper reason for being in business than making money, you are able to use this to navigate the process of growing your business. Because you are more focused on the bigger picture, this can help you stay on track and spot the right opportunities.

HELPS YOU ATTRACT YOUR IDEAL CLIENTS

Aligning with your purpose can help you attract your ideal clients. When you communicate your purpose it will be clear who you work with, and why. Your dream customers will respond to this. They will feel compelled to work with you and buy your products because they believe in what you are doing.

CAN ENABLE YOU TO HAVE A POSITIVE IMPACT IN THE WORLD

No matter how big or small your business is, you can make your mark on the world. Through your business, you can have a positive impact on your community. You can improve the local economy, help others with your services, or fight for a cause you believe in, as Erin Giles has done with End Sex Trafficking Day[2].

WHAT

WHAT RESULTS DO YOU GET?
WHAT DO YOU DO?
WHAT PRODUCTS AND SERVICES DO YOU OFFER?

HOW DOES WHAT YOU DO MAKE YOU SPECIAL?

HOW

HOW DOES YOUR PROCESS/WORKFLOW SET YOU APART?
HOW DO YOU DO WHAT YOU DO?

WHY DOES YOUR BUSINESS EXIST?

WHY

PURPOSE, CAUSE, OR BELIEF

"Thinking that the purpose of business is to MAKE MONEY is like thinking that human beings ARE ON THIS EARTH TO EAT. Eating allows us to fulfill our purpose in life and it is the same for business. PROFIT allows BUSINESS to make good on its GREATER PURPOSE."

JOHN MACKEY, founder of *Whole Foods Market*

"People don't buy WHAT you do; they buy WHY you do it."

SIMON SINEK

HOW TO FIND PURPOSE AND MEANING IN YOUR WORK

Understanding your business purpose is a necessary part of the process of defining your business, so you can go on to achieve success. Identifying the "why" of your business is not as complicated as it sounds, but it does require you to go deeper than the surface reasons you are telling yourself you're starting a business for.

Many creative entrepreneurs struggle with this. They consider the benefits of being in business rather than the reason *why* they are in it. This is short sighted and won't work. It won't help drive you when times get hard, when you are struggling to get your first client, or having to deal with low sales and even lower profits. Your purpose has to come from your core—a deeper place within you that motivates you to help others.

There is really only one question you need to ask to find your purpose and that is: *Why are you doing this*?

Most entrepreneurs often don't go deep enough when asked this question. They will answer with "because I want to make money," or, " I want to spend more time with my children." Those aren't reasons to have a business. If you want more money, you could get a better-paid job. If you want to spend more time with your children, get a part-time job so you can earn money and have the free time you desire to spend with your family.

Running a business and growing it into a successful one is demanding. You will likely work more hours than you ever did for someone else. Depending on your business, it may be harder to take time off for holidays or when you get sick. It could also be a few years before you start making a regular income. If your reasons for starting a business are weak, then you won't have a reason not to quit when the tough times come. Your purpose gives you a reason to struggle on through the difficult periods.

GETTING STARTED WITH FINDING YOUR PURPOSE

The process of finding and developing the deeper purpose of your business starts with asking yourself the following questions:

- Why are you doing this?
- Why do you want to be a business owner?
- Why did you choose this business idea and not another?

- Why do you offer what you do?
- Why should people be interested in what you provide?
- Why should people care about what you are offering?
- Why do you get excited about this business?

These questions will help you get started thinking about the deeper reason for being in business. They will help you understand what matters to you and what makes you tick; from here you can incorporate these values and beliefs into your business.

Another way to find your purpose is by using the purpose equation identified by Jess Lively[3]. While Jess relates this to an individual's purpose, it can be just as helpful for business owners to go through this process to find their purpose. It doesn't need you to try and look too deeply into what motivates you, rather it combines what you are doing in your business now (your talents) with how you help people (making them confident, helping their business grow, making them feel happy and content, teaching them something, and so on). The equation is simply: *your talents + helping people = your purpose*.

For example: *photography (your talent) + making women feel more confident (your way of helping people) = your purpose*

Your business purpose doesn't have to be a grandiose plan involving fame and recognition. You don't need your business to be the next TOMS, or for you to become the next Oprah to make a difference—every day people and businesses can have a remarkable impact on the world and on their clients, just by helping people in the way they know how.

Your business can help your customers and clients with something deeper than just selling them things. Whatever your business is, you can find an opportunity to bring purpose into the scenario:

Jewelry designer + helping women feel more beautiful = purpose

Graphic designer + helping small businesses feel professional = purpose

Cake decorator + helping parents to bring joy to their children's birthday parties = purpose

YOUR TALENTS
+ HELPING PEOPLE

= YOUR PURPOSE

[3]Jess Lively (www.jesslively.com)

WRITING A PURPOSE STATEMENT

(2)

Once you have a clear idea of your purpose, you can consolidate it into a purpose statement that you can easily refer to. Your purpose is a single mission that drives your company toward success. It needs to be simple and straightforward to understand, so keeping it short (to no longer than a sentence) can help you remember it and relate it to others.

Your purpose states "this is what we're doing for others" and how you are doing it. It's inspiring and motivational because it connects to people on a deeper level. Your purpose statement should:

- Define your long-term aspirations.
- State why you are doing what you are doing.
- Explain the impact you want to make with your work and through your success.
- Define the purpose of your company and the impact you want to make/to have on the world around you.
- Share what you do for others.
- Explain why you get up and go to work every day.
- Set out what good you are aiming to do in the world. What lasting difference do you want to make?

Your purpose statement communicates what you do, who you do it for, how you do it, and why. In essence it states:

I (what you do) for (describe the people you serve) by (explain how you do it) because (why you do it).

There is no set way to write your purpose statement. The most important thing is that it covers the following points:

- Why you do what you do.
- Who you do it for.
- What impact you wish to make on the world.

Above all, your purpose statement needs to inspire you and others to want to be a part of the work you are doing.

DEFINING YOUR VISION

Running a creative business is about more than just making and selling. To be successful, it helps to have a vision; a bigger picture for what you want your business to achieve in the future. Having a vision prevents your business stagnating. It can propel you forward, and it can be a marker for success that is unrelated to external factors such as money or sales.

You might ask: *"Isn't that my mission statement? I already have one of those."*

You need a mission statement too, which explains where your business is now; what you currently provide, how you do this, and why. But a vision statement sets out where you hope your business will be in the future. It is what you *wish* to provide, how, and why.

For example, online marketplace Etsy's mission statement is: *To enable people to make a living making things and to reconnect makers with buyers.*

However, its vision is: *To build a new economy and to present a better choice.*

The mission statement is what they do now; the vision is what they wish to achieve in years to come.

Creating a vision statement is a three-step process:

1) DETERMINE YOUR VISION

Think about why you started your business. Was it to provide a handmade alternative to mass-produced products? Maybe you wanted to provide natural beauty products or fun and colorful organic toys for children? Whatever the reason, it's a starting point for your vision statement.

Now, where would you like your business to be in the future? Who will you be selling to and what products will you sell? Think about the world around you and how you can create your mark on the world with your business.

2) WRITE IT DOWN

Writing your vision down can help provide motivation. Keep it short and memorable, and refer back to it often.

3) PUT IT INTO ACTION

To make your vision a reality you need to live and breathe it. Etsy's vision is inherent in all it does, and is part of its philosophy. Use your vision to guide your business planning and make sure your goals are working toward it.

DEFINING YOUR CORE VALUES

Core values are the rules you do business by. They are part of your company's DNA, defining what your business stands for, representing your guiding principles, and supporting your vision of who you wish to do business with. Your core values can help customers recognize whether you are a "good fit" for them because they reflect what you value as a person—and people do business with people they understand and relate to. Your values also help clients understand what you are about and who you are as a company.

However, you can't just set any values—they have to be things you already hold near. You just need to discover and define them.

When I started my first business, I wanted to show that marketing could be done in a different way—that it could be authentic, relationship centered, and based on engagement and interaction. I wanted to be transparent and for the business to be full of who I was.

Those are my values, which act as an internal barometer by which I can measure all business decisions. When I was deciding whether a client was a good fit, I revisited my values. Diversifying into teaching online classes? I went back to my values to create a course that I knew in my heart was the right thing, instead of what was expected of me. Whatever the business decision, I want it to be in line with what I personally believe to be right for me at that time.

HONEST
ETHICAL
STRONG
NATURAL
GENEROUS
ECO-FRIENDLY

Rather than limiting my business, knowing my core values helps make my business stronger. It means I'm not swayed by what my competitors are doing, and I can consistently connect with my ideal clients because we find value in the same things. I can use my own voice and put my heart into my business without feeling pressure to be or do something different.

Your customers will seek out people that have similar values to them. It's becoming increasingly common to connect with a business first before making a purchase. The "about" page on a website is one of the most visited pages for a reason—people want to know what you and your business stand for. The words you use and your brand messaging should communicate this both consistently and authentically.

Your business values are not something you can copy from someone else or follow from a blueprint. The values must mean something to you personally, or it will come across as contrived or artificial.

A great example of a business using values to guide it is The Green Gables[4]. Owner, Gabrielle Treanor, has strong ethical and green values that she highlights on her website. She says it was natural to build a business on her personal values, and this has also helped her diversify into other products, while remaining true to her brand.

As Gabrielle explains: "Strong values can definitely be a driving force. I don't just want to make and sell pretty looking stationery—I want to give consumers the option to buy responsibly produced stationery that shows there's a market for recycling paper and gives them a great-looking product without them compromising on quality or price. This is what spurs me on and keeps me motivated."

HOW CAN YOU IDENTIFY YOUR CORE VALUES?

START WITH YOU

What personal values do you hold at your core? What is important to you? Use these core values to build the foundation of your brand.

WHAT IS YOUR PERSONAL MISSION FOR YOUR BUSINESS?

Why do you want to do what you do? Who are you trying to help and why? Refer back to your purpose statement—what values come from that?

HOW DO YOU WANT YOUR AUDIENCE TO PERCEIVE YOUR BUSINESS?

What are the most important parts of your story that you want to share with them? Show them you fit into their lives and have a similar value system.

Whenever (and wherever) you decide to grow your business, these values should stay at the center of everything you do. They are timeless and don't change because they are inherent in your business and core being.

[4]Gabrielle Treanor (www.thegreengables.co.uk)

DECIDING WHO YOU WILL SERVE

②

Deciding who you're going to serve with your business is essential to ongoing success. The people you serve are your target market; the people you'll be creating products and services for. Before you can serve them, you need to have a clear idea of who they are and how you can help them. Sometimes called a "niche," your target market is a smaller segment of the overall market; a smaller piece of a bigger pie.

Say, for example, you are selling sketchbooks. Instead of trying to sell them to everyone who can use a pencil, you could concentrate on selling to artists. You can then segment the niche even further depending on your product. If your sketchbook has a pocket in the back that is great for storing bits of found paper, then you could target mixed-media artists or artists who use vintage or found paper. It might seem crazy limiting your market this way, but you can then focus all your efforts on a target market that is most likely to buy your product *and* is willing to part with the cash for it.

When you have found your niche, you can share the benefits of your products and the message will be understood. You will be able to connect and engage with them on a whole new level because your product fits into their lives. The market will still be large enough to provide you a great income, and you will be able to find a role in that market as you are very clear on what you provide.

So who is your true target market? (Hint: they might not be who you think they are.)

- Your true target market is ready to buy your product now.
- It is willing to pay what your product is worth.
- The benefit of your product is something the target market needs or wants.

FINDING YOUR TARGET MARKET

If there's a target market for your product or service, the next step is to find it. This means looking at two things:

LOOK AT PAST CUSTOMERS
Look at commonalities between the people that have bought your products so far. This takes time and a bit of investigation, but

you don't need to over-complicate it. Only consider what is relevant to your product.

If you normally interact with your customers via social media, you should already know a lot about them. If you'd like to know more then you could create a survey for them to complete, or ask if they would like to take part in a focus group to discuss how your products are benefiting them. If they have a blog/website/their own shop/Twitter account, then read through and look at common things they write about. All this information will give you a general idea about who loves your work and who is willing to pay for it.

LOOK AT YOUR PRODUCT

Who really needs it? What are the benefits of using your product over someone else's? Does it have a defining feature or selling point; either a physical or emotional benefit to the user?

Who is *really* going to buy it? People are different. You may want every 25–35 year old woman in the country to wear your handmade jewelry, but are they *all* really going to want your product? Even within a specific age group or income level, people have different tastes and preferences. The key is finding out what those are so you can ensure you aim your product at the right people.

Remember, if you are aiming at everybody, you are aiming at no one.

You are looking for the people who value handmade AND can afford it. Forget about targeting people who love your product, but have no money. They might love what you make, but ultimately they won't buy it.

Once you know your true target market you can use this information to drive your advertising, promotion, product development, and guide your prices.

So that sketchbook that is perfect for mixed-media artists? Well, aim your promotional activity at them, honing your message so that those artists know that your product is right for them. If you have an advertising budget, advertise where this segment of the market will be frequenting. When it comes to developing new products, think about solving a problem for this range of people that are already your fans.

Finding your true target market is like gold dust. When you know who the true fans of your product are, everything else will fall into place. These people will be passionate about what you do and will spread the word to their like-minded friends. As a result, selling will no longer be a struggle and your business will be able to grow.

BUILD THE
FOUNDATION

3

WHY YOU NEED A STRONG FOUNDATION

Planning for your business is best done from the ground up, just as building a house starts with a solid foundation to construct on. A business has lots of moving parts, all of which need to go on top of the foundation, so your business is only ever as strong as the foundation you build it on. The stronger it is, the more stability there will be to grow in the long term while sustaining shifts in the economy or societal changes. A weak foundation, however, leaves your business vulnerable to external challenges and can even put you out of business altogether.

The foundation of your business is made up of the systems and procedures that you undertake when you start out. These are things that, when done properly, can make your business stronger—managing your day-to-day tasks, structuring your day, and how you get things done, for example.

Jumping straight into designing a logo and trying to market your product will mean you start out with a weak foundation, pushing your products on the wrong people because you didn't take the time at the beginning to do the work. A business that has laid a strong foundation will not need to force marketing—you won't need to shout at people to get your message heard. Instead, you will easily connect and engage with potential customers because they will recognize how your products can help them.

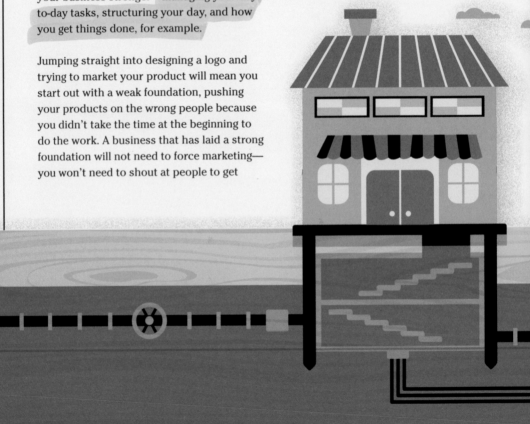

BUILDING YOUR BUSINESS FOUNDATION

FOCUS ON THE LONG TERM

You can't be short-sighted in business. Consider your long-term goals and the results you want to achieve.

SET FINANCIAL GOALS

How much capital do you need to start up? How much money do you need to make? How much of that is profit? You need to be clear what you want to achieve financially so you have something to aim for and stay on track.

ASSESS MARKET CONDITIONS

Is there really a need for your business? How does it fit into the current market landscape? If your business isn't providing a need for people who can afford to spend money on what you are offering, then you'll need to consider how you can adapt your idea to make it stronger.

CONSIDER YOUR SKILL SET

Be honest about your skills and talents. If you really can't design, you shouldn't become a designer! Look at the competition and consider whether your skills are really on a par with them. Can you really compete with them? Don't build a business on a skill you don't possess.

BE AWARE OF WHAT IS HAPPENING IN YOUR INDUSTRY

In order to stay ahead of the competition you need to be up to date with what's happening in your industry. What trends and insights can you glean? Even if you're not trend focused with your products, the trends will still affect how people buy. How will these trends impact on your business? Are there trade shows or other industry events you can go to or magazines you can subscribe to that can keep you informed of current issues?

IMPLEMENTATION

Once you have your business strategy in place, make sure you implement it and do it well. If you aren't able to fulfill some of the necessary tasks, hire someone who can do them for you. You also want to make sure you don't always work on daily tasks, but also spend time working on the business itself. Stick to your business plan and remain focused on your goals.

HAVE A MONEY BACK UP PLAN

If possible, try and save enough money to see you through at least a few months. This will help if sales are slow or a client doesn't pay on time.

CREATING A BUSINESS MODEL THAT WORKS FOR YOU

Building a creative business can come with its ups and downs. Not everyone understands why or how we do it—being an artist, designer, crafter, or maker is still seen as unconventional by many. Society informs us that we haven't achieved anything unless we fulfill its criteria of success, which usually involves generating millions in revenue, becoming famous in your field, owning a huge house, and driving a flashy car. But success might mean something different to you, and it is important that you begin building your empire with a business model that works for you.

When it comes to determining success—including what it means to you and how you wish to achieve it—you will be bombarded with opinions that can leave you feeling unsure, isolated, or even as if you are a failure. Success for creative entrepreneurs does not need to have the same definition as for other business owners. In fact, the definition of success for you and your business, can and should be defined by *you*. No business is the same. We all bring different experiences and life stories into the mix, which will impact on what we individually want or need success to be.

- What do you want to achieve?
- What is success to you?

You may need to earn "X" amount per month to enable you to keep following your dream, and you might dream of your products becoming famous and of all the money that may bring. There is nothing wrong with that. We each decide what path to follow and what is best for ourselves and the people who mean something to us.

When it comes to business growth, there really is no "one size fits all" approach. Every business has a lot of moving parts, so what works for one expanding business may not be the same thing that will take yours to the next level. A freelance graphic designer will need a vastly different business model to a boutique stationery studio, for example, while a gluten-free cupcake baker will employ an approach that is contrary to that of a custom wedding dress designer, and a specialty artisan bakery owner needs a business model greatly varied from that of a fine artist. You get the idea.

Even within that, two artisan bakers may develop different business models. One might decide to have a small bakery where they can sell to customers directly, perhaps with a cafe so they can get income from selling fair-trade coffee and specialty teas in addition to their breads and pastries.

Another baker might decide they want to supply larger bakeries or sell to giant supermarket chains. They might not have a customer facing store at all and instead concentrate on building their brand within their niche and building relationships with other businesses. Both models could be lucrative, depending on their goals, values, vision, and overall purpose for their business.

WHAT DOES YOUR IDEAL DAY LOOK LIKE?

If you are struggling to decide which direction to take your business model, determining your ideal day can help. How you want to spend your day will help you hone in on what business model will work best for you. If you want to have your products in thousands of stores, then you can look into wholesaling to retailers or licensing your products.

Or maybe you don't envisage making your products at all. You might want to keep the designer role, but outsource production. This is a different business model, and you will need to find production staff and suppliers. So what would *your* ideal day look like when you are running your business?

WHO WOULD YOU SPEND IT WITH?
Will you work mostly alone or with a team?

WHAT WOULD YOU DO?
What business tasks would you undertake? Will you delegate tasks to team members and professionals? Will you do your own accounting, photography, and website development? Can you see yourself doing these things as part of your role?

WHERE WOULD YOU GO?
Do you have a studio or retail shop? Are you working from home? Do you sell online? Do you work from the beach?

WOULD YOU SPEND A WORK DAY DIFFERENTLY THAN A NON-WORK DAY?
What would you do in your downtime? Would you prefer lots of free time for hobbies, friends, and family? Would you be happier working intensely for a few years? Working with large retailers and establishments might mean you have to work to their deadlines—would you mind that?

DEFINING YOUR BUSINESS STRUCTURE

There are a number of business entity options for your company. Each one has different benefits and drawbacks in terms of how easy they are to form, manage, and the cost to get it done legally. While choosing your business structure might not be as exciting as the nitty-gritty task of business building, it still needs to be done correctly, or you could be breaking the law. Every country and state is different, so the best advice is to seek professional advice from your local county court or council.

HOW TO SELECT THE RIGHT COMPANY STRUCTURE FOR YOU

Before you jump in to selecting a company structure, consider the goals and vision for your business, so you can ensure that you choose the type of business that will be best for you. The following entities apply to the USA, but many countries have similar—if not identical—business categories.

SOLE PROPRIETORSHIP

A sole proprietorship exists when a single individual owns a business and all its assets. There is no distinction made between you and the business, so you can simply claim all the profits and declare it on your personal tax form. You will be liable for any losses or debts your business accrues, so if your business is sued by an unhappy client, they may have a right to claim your personal property.

If you are doing business as a sole proprietor, and there is even a small chance that you could be sued, then you should have business insurance. For a relatively minimal fee you

can have some peace of mind, in case a product you supply hurts someone (even inadvertently), or the service you provide brings harm to your customer.

Operating a sole proprietorship business can be done under your legal name or under a business name you create. This is often called a "fictitious name" or a "DBA" ("doing business as"). You will need to fill out an "assumed name certificate," which declares that you as an individual will be operating a business under that name.

GENERAL PARTNERSHIP

A general partnership is essentially the same as a sole proprietorship, except it involves two or more people. It will therefore require a contract or agreement between all of the parties concerned.

As with a sole proprietorship, you and your partner(s) are liable for any business debts as your business will not be considered a separate entity. A general partnership doesn't provide any protection for company debts, even if only one partner has signed the contract. For that reason, you need to make sure you trust your partner and get separate legal advice before you go into a partnership agreement.

Some states permit a limited liability partnership (LLP) as an alternative, which offers greater protection from the actions of other partners.

LIMITED LIABILITY COMPANY (LLC)

If you have plans to one day sell your company, you may prefer to structure your business as an LLC. This forms the company as a separate legal entity, so it is easily transferred to new owners. An LLC also provides limited liability to its directors and is often considered the easiest form of incorporated business to run. It has less paperwork than traditional corporations and is easy to form.

In most states, you form an LLC with the Secretary of State or the commerce division in your state. If you are unsure, employ the help of a business attorney.

③

CHOOSING THE RIGHT NAME FOR YOUR BUSINESS

One of the hardest things when starting a business is choosing a business name that feels right. It always seems like all the best ones are taken, and even if you do find one with the domain name available, the social media handles have been taken (usually by someone who only used them once way back in 2010!). It can feel so unfair!

Naming your business sets the tone and defines what you offer, so there is a lot of pressure to get it right. However, there is no secret formula to choosing the right business name. There are millions of businesses with what could be considered terrible names, and yet they have still managed to make it work for them. A name doesn't just arrive perfectly out of thin air—it only becomes a good name when it starts to mean something.

PAINLESSLY CHOOSE A BUSINESS NAME

Naming a business doesn't need to be hard. Go with your gut, you will know when you find the right name.

BUILDING A PERSONAL BRAND

Are you working one-on-one with people, writing books, or offering creative services as an expert in your field? Maybe you are a fashion designer or life coach? If you're trying to build a personal brand, try using your name. It will be different and you'll be able to peg your brand onto it.

LOOK TO THE FUTURE

Do you hope to sell the business one day, or will it always be just you? If you have plans to sell it on, maybe reconsider choosing your own name as your brand name.

DREAM BIG

Beware of limiting yourself to a name that can't cross into other areas later on. If you

42

call your business *Nourish Lunches*, for example, it might be difficult to expand into other areas, as you'll always be associated with lunches.

DON'T RUSH IT

When you find a name you like, think on it for a while before sharing it with the world. This gives you a chance to test it out on family and friends first. Use the new name in conversation to see if it feels, sounds, and looks right when written down.

BE FLEXIBLE

If you can't get the domain you want, add another word, take a letter off, or add a letter. If your perfect social media username is in use, get inventive. However, if another brand offering is very similar, it is usually best to steer clear.

DO YOUR RESEARCH

Check domains, trademarks, search engines, and social media sites to see if your name has been taken. Some are more important than others.

USE A PHRASE OR STATEMENT

Your company name doesn't have to be short. While one or two words can keep it simple, choosing a phrase or a statement can help you stand out and show off an unconventional personality. It can also be easier to remember a phrase rather than a random word or two, as a phrase will evoke a feeling or emotion. It's also more likely that the name will be available, which means no trademark issues. You will also have lots of room to work with when it comes to branding, naming your services, and creating a fun and lively brand personality. Examples

of this type of name include *I can't believe it's not butter* and *Seven for all mankind*.

GET INSPIRATION

You can use the dictionary, thesaurus, short stories, poems, symbolism from different cultures, or past history. Don't think you need to find a word that means something—find words that *remind you of something* instead.

DON'T MAKE IT HARD FOR YOUR CUSTOMERS

Choose real words. Made-up words are harder to remember and attach a feeling or emotion to. Choose something that's easy to spell and pronounce—remember that people need to be able to read it, say it, and search for it online. Also, ask yourself if the name will be easy to find online? If you are using words that are common, or there are too many other similar business names, you may want to choose something else.

Also note that names containing multiple numbers are tricky for people to remember. For example "417 studio" might be confused with "741 studio" until the brand becomes established. This is an avoidable barrier to brand recognition.

STUCK? GET PROFESSIONAL HELP

If you get really stuck, use a naming service. Most freelance copywriters can help you choose a name. Copywriters know the business of words, so you can work with them to find the perfect name to express your new business or product.

THE ONE-PAGE BUSINESS PLAN

I'm going to let you into a little secret. You probably don't need a business plan—at least not in the traditional sense. Unless you are seeking outside investment, you really don't need a 40+ page business plan that you will never look at again once you've written it.

A business plan is just that—a plan for your business. It is a roadmap for how you are going to implement your business model. So start with that and plan out the essentials. It doesn't have to be pages long, with financial projections, profit-and-loss statements, and your team resumes—you will be working with it, so you need to want to look at it.

DOING IT YOUR WAY

For your business plan you can do lots of research and go into each topic in depth, or you can use it as a brief framework. You can also make it work for you by thinking about how you process information best. Are you visual? Or do you prefer things written out?

You can write your business plan in long form; in bullet points; sketch it; or even collage bits of magazine clippings onto a big sheet of paper—whatever it takes for you to get the answers to these questions out of your head and into some kind of organized plan to work from.

Take each subject one item at a time and schedule a set time each week to tackle a part of the plan, or tackle a few items a day. This way, it gets done in manageable chunks and you won't get overwhelmed.

Write the business plan in your voice—you will be working from it, so you need to recognize yourself in it.

Also, remember your business plan is not set in stone. All businesses evolve over time, especially creative ones. Your interests might change or you may adapt the business later on, depending on what your customers need and want from you.

BUSINESS PLAN CHECKLIST

1. BUSINESS OVERVIEW..........

2. TARGET MARKET................

3. COMPETITORS .... ☐

4. YOUR TEAM............................ ☐

5. MARKETING PLAN .... ☐

6. BUSINESS SYSTEMS............. ☐

7. MONEY .... ☐

WHAT TO INCLUDE IN YOUR ONE-PAGE BUSINESS PLAN

BUSINESS OVERVIEW (EXECUTIVE SUMMARY)

How are you going to make money? What will you sell? What is your business purpose, mission, and vision? Keep your overview short and to the point.

TARGET CUSTOMERS/ IDEAL CLIENTS

This is where you will explain who your business is targeting, who your ideal clients are, and who will actually buy what you sell. Is there a need or market for it?

COMPETITION/ COMPETITIVE ADVANTAGE

Who are your main competitors? What makes your idea better or different from theirs? You can go into some of their strengths and weaknesses, but the main thing is to look at the opportunities that their failings bring you. What can you do better than them? Is there anything missing that you think your target market deserves, or that would make it easier for them to receive your particular service or product?

HUMAN RESOURCES

What staff will you need to run your business? These could be employees or freelancers who you team up with to provide a larger range of services. If you are working alone, you can leave this part out.

MARKETING PLAN

How are you going to tell your potential clients about what you do? How will you communicate with them? How will you get your products and services in front of them?

OPERATIONS

What are your business processes? How will you get the job done in the most efficient way? The systems that you use can make or break your business, so make sure you have a defined process to make your products or gain new clients. Work through every step to see where you can make improvements.

FINANCIAL

How much money do you need to get started? How are you going to make money? Will you be selling products or services? If so, which ones? What are the profit margins on each product? You need to know how much profit you will make from each sale. Also consider other streams of income you make.

While I don't think you need pages and pages of profit-and-loss statements, you do need to know how much product or how many service packages you need to sell to make a profit and keep you on track to earn the income you desire.

The easiest way to do this is to work backward from the annual income you would like. For example, if you are a designer and aim to earn $100,000 per year, how many design clients will you need to take on per month? Is that feasible?

LU & ED

WHO: Cody Bauchman
WHAT: Stuffed plush monsters
WEBSITE: www.luanded.com

Before starting my business, I was afraid of...

Missing out on seeing my son grow up. I had worked full time outside the home since I was aged 17, and for the first three years of my son's life. This meant I missed his first steps, the first time he crawled, and so many other "firsts." I saw this as an opportunity to depart from the corporate world and fulfill my dream of being a work-from-home mother, so I could always be present for my son. It was the best choice I ever made!

The one thing I wish I had known before starting my business...

Is how difficult it is to find a community that is kind, supportive, and genuine. After joining many catty and ruthless "craft communities" I finally found a real community for creatives at ohmyhandmade. com. It is such a positive and warm environment where I truly feel safe to share about my life, my business, my struggles, and successes. I feel like every person out there starting out on their creative business journey needs to find a community they feel safe to share in, where they can reach out for help and receive support, or where their success stories are celebrated with their fellow community members, not picked apart with snarky or jealous comments.

My best tip for new creative business owners...

It doesn't happen overnight, or in a week, or a month, or maybe even in a year or more. Finding "success"—whatever your definition of it is—takes hard work and perseverance. You have to be so many things: a CEO, the head of marketing, the head of PR, market analyst, researcher, product tester, production manager, scheduler, creator, strategist, bookkeeper, sales rep, social media manager, and so much more.

My favorite thing about running my own business...

Being home with my son. I have loved watching him grow and being able to show him you really can be anything you want to be—even something as silly as a monster maker!

4

CREATE ACTIONABLE GOALS AND INTENTIONS

HOW TO SET AUDACIOUS GOALS

Goals are something you aim for and they can be as big or as small as you wish. Some people like setting goals, and see it as a clear path to feeling happy about what they have achieved. Others don't like it, because if you don't meet your goals it can be a reminder that you don't measure up.

When it comes to setting effective goals for growth, you need to ensure you have some clarity about what you would like to achieve. After considering where you are now with your money, income streams, and marketing, you should have a better idea of where there is room for improvement and where you want to be. How you decide to grow your business is a personal choice—it's up to you to decide what is important to you and how you will achieve it.

It's also up to you to decide what success looks like for you, and how you will recognize it when you get there. Everyone has different desires and things going on in their lives, and this can impact on what you think you can get done.

However, don't let other people's ideas of success get in the way of what you really want. If you want your business to stay small and personal, go for it. Alternatively, if you want to grow your business into a global brand, with your products found on the shelves of some of the world's biggest department stores, then take the first step in the right direction—you can do it!

SMART GOAL SETTING

Using the acronym SMART will allow you to determine a set of clear goals that you can work toward. SMART stands for:

- Specific
- Measurable
- Achievable
- Realistic
- Timely

So, if you wanted to gain more features in the press you might set a SMART goal of:

Contact six magazine editors over the next three months by email with my press kit.

This goal is **specific** because it says exactly what you will do.

It is **measurable** because you will be able to look back to see if you achieved that number.

It is **achievable** and **realistic** because you have given yourself enough time to reach the goal (contacting two editors a month).

It is **timely** because you have given yourself a date to have completed it by. This will help keep you on track and accountable.

Setting goals like this will be much more effective than simply saying "I want to achieve more press," and it's important to set goals for your business before you get started. Having goals to work toward can not only help you make a success of your business, but the process of setting goals forces you to think about what you want to get out of your business, what success looks like to you, and which directions you can go in to achieve that.

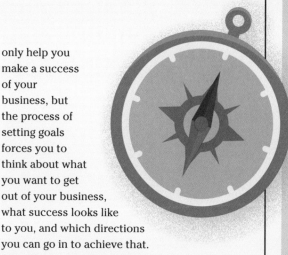

CREATING YOUR GOALS

1) What are your goals? Where do you want to go with your business?

2) Turn these into goal statements, such as "I want to create a new range of art prints," or "I want to earn a profit of $4,000 a month."

3) Break each goal down into achievable steps by brainstorming an action list for each.

4) Put the action points in order of how you will do them. I find it easiest to start from where I want to be, then work backward. Going back to the art print example, a list of action points might look like this:

- Brainstorm image ideas.
- Research what is already out there.
- Find inspiration for the collection.
- Buy paper, ink, and packaging materials.
- Plan a photoshoot.
- Write a product listing and list them on my website.
- Devise a promotional strategy.

5) For each point, write out further actions to take within them. What needs to be done to devise your promotional strategy, for example, or where can you look for inspiration? Write as much as you can for each step, until you have a list to work from. This will become your "to do" list. Put the steps in order of when each one needs to be done, then work from that list to get them done.

TAKING ACTION ON YOUR GOALS

We can spend our whole lives waiting for things to be perfect before we actually do something. We read up on as much as we can, we plan, we strategize, we dream, and we hope. But if you don't take action, then you might as well have done nothing—you won't have actually achieved anything. The best strategy in the world won't work if you don't implement it, and no amount of research or planning will help you become a success if you don't action it.

To prevent all your learning from being a waste, you need to create a roadmap for action; a plan you can follow to reach your goals with realistic strategies to help you get over any roadblocks you might encounter in the future.

By now you should have an idea of what direction you wish to go. Your ideas may not be fleshed out, but you should have an idea of where you see yourself in the future. To bring your vision to life, you need to take action— this is what moves you forward.

WHAT IS AN ACTION PLAN?

An action plan is a strategy or outline of what you need to do to complete your goals. Each goal will have a number of steps that need to be completed, and your action plan will guide you and give you something to work toward. This makes everything you do for your business more intentional than just hoping for the best.

An action plan can also help you stay focused, enable you to prioritize the things that need to get done, and identify those steps that will make a bigger impact. To get started, ask yourself the following questions:

- What are my three most important goals?
- What gets in the way and prevents me from achieving these goals?
- Do I have any fears or emotional blocks that tell me I can't—or shouldn't—achieve my goals?
- Do I have an effective productivity model in place?
- What are the two (or three) action steps I can take this week to get closer to the completion of each of my goals?
- What support system do I have in place? (This could be an assistant, business partner, coach, or mentor.)

ACTION PLAN SPECIFICS

BREAK DOWN YOUR GOALS INTO THEMES OR SIMILAR SUBJECTS

Identify the main things you want to accomplish and group them together—promotional goals, product development goals, personal development goals, and so on. Ask yourself what you need to reach each goal and how you will know when you have achieved it.

PRIORITIZE YOUR GOALS

Which ones are the most important for you at this moment? Which ones do you absolutely have to do to reach your overall aims? This could be create new products or think up a business name, for example. Put your goals in order of which ones need to be completed first. These smaller goals will ultimately get you to your final big goal. What is the logical order for your goals and tasks? Put them in order of importance.

BRAINSTORM

Take each goal and brainstorm a list of all the things that need to be done to implement that goal. What are the different strategies you can use to promote your business more? How can you devise a remarkable product range that your target market will love? How can you get the help you need for your business? What areas do you need help with—do you need assistance with childcare, organization, promotional help, photography, or graphic design, for example?

PRIORITIZE TASKS

Prioritize your list of tasks the same way as you did your goals—in order of importance. Do you need to get a graphic designer first, or can you do that later? Do you need to work on your product offerings or service packages before changing your website?

CREATE A TIMELINE

For each task, work out a realistic timeline of when you can get each goal completed. This doesn't have to be set in stone (flexibility is key), but having something to work toward will help you stay focused on the task at hand. Divide the list up into weekly and monthly tasks.

STAY ACCOUNTABLE

Check in with a mentor or find a creative entrepreneur support group to keep you accountable. If you have client work, you will need to stay on track, but personal goals can sometimes end up getting put off forever and never get completed. If you are planning a launch or new product range, tell people when it will be—this can also motivate you to get things done.

CELEBRATE!

I recommend celebrating even small accomplishments—it will help keep you motivated and focused on achieving your bigger goals.

"Vision without
action is a
DAYDREAM.
Action without
vision is a
NIGHTMARE."

JAPANESE PROVERB

5

BRAND YOUR
BUSINESS

WHAT IS BRANDING?

Branding isn't design, and it's not your logo—it's much more than that. In fact, the visual design element (which is the part most people think of when you say "branding") comes much later in the process.

Branding is everything about your business that communicates a message to your potential customers. It is not just the things you can see, feel, or touch, such as your packaging or color palette, but it's also things you can't touch—customer service and perception, for example.

When you create a brand for your business you are expressing what your business stands for. A customer is more likely to return for repeat business if your brand speaks to them on some level. It is also easier to promote your business to your target market if you know clearly what your brand represents and who it will resonate with the most.

As an independent business, it can be hard to feel visible amongst established companies. It can feel as though you are a little fish in a big pond, with no one taking any notice of you. In order to stand out from the crowd it is essential that you brand your business in a way that will help it stand apart from the competition. If your brand identity is too similar to a rival's, your business will simply blend in. For example, if there are certain things that every company in your industry does (without reason) then you may want to avoid it. For example, Eco-friendly companies gravitate toward using a green and brown color palette—could you use a different color

instead? You will immediately stand out as doing things differently and your business will be easier to remember.

The first step in building an engaging brand isn't the design of your logo—it's unearthing the meaning behind who you are, what you believe in, and why you do what you do. That's your story. Sure, a strong logo and beautiful website are important to success, but an effective, engaging, memorable brand tells a story that people want to hear, and more importantly, want to share.

You then condense your story down to the basics, choosing three to five brand tone words that express how you want your brand to feel. These tone words give direction to the design stage, and can also be used to guide your marketing voice.

Whether you know much about branding or not, you are already a brand. A brand is the impression you leave on people, whether that's you as an individual or your business. While your logo is a symbol that represents your business, your brand is what's underneath—your business' personality.

Many people think about what they want their brand to look like, before they consider how they want to make people feel, missing out the most important step. Strong, powerful brands work because they evoke feeling: we remember them because of how they made us feel. And if you are clear about your brand, that makes it easier for you to communicate it effectively to the people that matter.

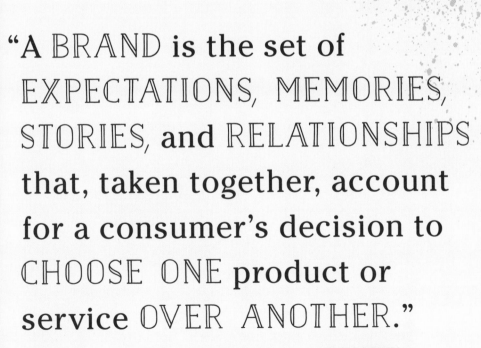

"A BRAND is the set of EXPECTATIONS, MEMORIES, STORIES, and RELATIONSHIPS that, taken together, account for a consumer's decision to CHOOSE ONE product or service OVER ANOTHER."

SETH GODIN

HOW TO USE BRANDING EFFECTIVELY

Your brand is a reflection of what you stand for, so it has to align perfectly with the values and purpose of your business. The overall aim of branding is to inspire trust within your ideal client so they feel compelled to buy from you. In the same way that celebrities have fans that will buy whatever branded product they release, you want to create a consistent image and reputation so that the people you are trying to attract will buy your products from you. Using branding effectively will help you instill that trust.

One of the most important aspects of branding is continuity. Branding brings together your business vision, purpose, and values. It needs to be consistent and express these values so that people can understand what to expect if they work with you or buy your products. Making sure that you present the same message on all brand touchpoints can be tricky unless you define and stick to a brand strategy. Your brand strategy can ensure you communicate your brand in the same way on your business cards, website, advertisements, and in person.

GETTING STARTED

BRAND MESSAGE

In order to determine your brand identity you first need to decide what you want your brand to communicate. This is known as your "brand message" (or "brand purpose"), which reflects the values and promise of your business that you want to convey to potential customers. Is your business quirky and fun, or luxurious and exclusive? You should be able to sum up your brand message in one sentence and it will go on to guide the rest of your branding strategy. For example: "We create natural children's products that are also fun and colorful."

BRAND VALUES

These are core values that your company represents. They also act as a benchmark to measure all business activities against. Examples include words such as *natural, quality, trustworthy,* and *organic.*

BRAND PROMISE

This is the statement you make to customers that identifies what they should expect from all interactions with your company and products. It covers what you stand for, and also promises something relevant to your potential customers. Your brand promise is a combination of what your brand cares about the most, what your target customers actually want, and what your competitors are not offering.

BE AUTHENTIC

Your brand promise is something that customers will consistently expect, so you will have to be able to deliver. There is no point trying to be something you're not—consumers are sophisticated and will spot a fraud a mile off. Make sure your brand reflects you, that it's authentic and real, and above all, make sure it is *true.*

CONSISTENCY IS KEY

Once you've decided on your branding, it is important to follow this through and use it for all aspects of your business' visual and non-visual communication. Your website, packaging, and products all need to work together to communicate your brand message. So, if you are selling a luxury product, don't confuse this message by offering regular cut-price sales.

Make sure your brand messaging is consistently delivered at every customer touchpoint, be it through the quality of your product or service, your packaging, logos, tag line, and all of your marketing materials.

(5)

IMAGE IS EVERYTHING

When you are starting out, it can be tempting to save money by cutting corners. Don't! Using a cheaper option from the outset can damage your business or stop you from getting customers. If your visual brand looks unprofessional or amateurish you won't be able to instill trust and compete against the competition. Areas to pay attention to are:

PROFESSIONAL PACKAGING AND PROMOTIONAL MATERIALS

Would you trust a bespoke letterpress stationery company that couldn't afford to get decent quality business cards for itself? Of course not! Make sure you use the best materials you can afford, especially if you are in the business of selling those services to others.

BUSINESS BANK ACCOUNT WITH YOUR BRAND NAME

Imagine you are on the verge of securing a wholesale account with a global retailer and you ask for funds to be sent to your personal bank account? They might question how long you expect to be around if you are not taking yourself seriously; you may even lose the account. Set a business account up as soon as you can.

TRADEMARKS

Your products and services are a part of your brand. If you have coined a name for a new product, and don't want someone else to use it, get it trademarked. Yes, it can be costly, but it affords you protection and is worth it.

BRANDED EMAIL ADDRESS WITH YOUR BUSINESS NAME/DOMAIN NAME

Using a Hotmail or AOL email account looks unprofessional. Instead, use a Gmail account and use forward masking to have your domain name show up.

ALWAYS HAVE A DOMAIN NAME

Domains cost a few dollars a year. It is essential to secure your domain before you get started branding your business, even if you are only going to use it to forward to an Etsy shop, or other e-commerce site.

BRANDED SOCIAL MEDIA ACCOUNTS

If you are using Twitter for your business, use your brand name, and not a nickname— *Fluffybunny647* does not imply a professional web designer, for example!

SURVIVAL ORGANS

WHO: Vanessa Laven
WHAT: Plush internal organs
WEBSITE: www.mixedmartialartsandcrafts.com

Before starting my business, I was afraid of...

I was afraid of not selling a single item. I thought selling plush internal organs for cancer survivors might be too niche and that people wouldn't understand why I started Survival Organs. I was afraid of offending people because cancer is a touchy subject I was afraid that I would be the shop that would revive Regretsy, and was afraid of getting nasty emails telling me my stuff was no good.

The one thing I wish I had known before starting my business...

I wish I had known that I need to be busy in order to get things done. When I have all day to do something, it doesn't get done until the last possible moment. I wish I had known how important it is to do something—no matter how awful—just to get the idea out of my head and into my hands. I wish I had known how important innovation is. It's okay for things to grow and change over time—I don't need to have everything perfectly done off the bat.

My best tip for new creative business owners...

Stop talking and start doing! Even if it's ugly or not what you pictured, by having things done you're able to refine and edit. If your idea never gets out of the idea stage, you don't have a business. You have an idea. So go out there and make stuff—worry about how it looks later. Make now and edit when you're done!

My favorite thing about running my own business...

Is that I can determine the pace and path I'm taking. I can determine what needs an immediate deadline and what can be pushed back. I love that I get to choose what I work on and I don't have to do "busy work," like re-alphabetizing files that were already in order. I can take an hour-long lunch break if I really need to rest my eyes and my doctor's appointments don't count against me.

⑤

LEARN TO BE YOURSELF

Finding a point of difference between you and your competitors is easier than you think, although sometimes it can be difficult to discern what your unique selling point is. You may provide quality products that are unusual and different to what's on offer on the high street, but you're not the only one. When you start contacting the media for features they will want to know why they should feature you and not one of the other designer-makers out there. So what are you going to tell them?

YOU ARE YOUR USP

Instead of trying to force a USP, you simply need to look close to home to find out what makes your business different from your competitors: the unique selling point of your business, and the one element that can't be replicated by anyone else, is *YOU*. Your personality, your creativity, the way you approach things, even your dreams and vision—all of these help to make your business different from anyone else's.

Your input into your business is non-negotiable. Product ranges will come and go, and cash flow will rise and fall, but you are the one constant that ties all the strands of your business together. So, let's take a look at how you can get more "you" in your business.

LISTEN TO YOUR GUT

Your instincts are usually right. Only you know what is best for you, so it's time to start trusting yourself when it comes to making important decisions that will help to move your business forward.

PUT MORE OF YOUR PERSONALITY INTO YOUR PRODUCTS

Try not to be influenced by others when you create. The more of you there is in your products, the harder they will be to replicate.

BE YOURSELF WHEN FORGING CUSTOMER RELATIONSHIPS

Forcing yourself to be something you're not can make you seem false and untrustworthy. When you are yourself, your target market will understand that and want to connect with you.

SHARE YOUR STORY WHEN YOU ARE MARKETING AND PROMOTING YOUR BUSINESS

The path you took to get to this point is unique to you, so share it with the world.

CREATE BRANDING THAT REFLECTS WHO YOU ARE AND YOUR VALUES

What you believe in can be a great way to stand out from your competitors, so express it in your branding and everything else you do.

BE AUTHENTIC

Who you are is what makes you and your business special. Each and every one of us brings a different truth into this world.

Be proud of who you are and stay true to yourself. Allowing your soul to shine will help your business stand out from your competitors.

ALWAYS USE YOUR OWN VOICE

Initially, whenever I'd try to write really "clever" posts online on marketing and branding I'd attempt to write them in what I thought was a professional manner. The problem was that tone didn't come naturally to me, and it didn't show my personality. As soon as I started writing posts as though I was talking to a dear friend, it became easier to distinguish myself from others. Your voice is important, use it.

BE TRANSPARENT

Let people see you. The real you. Don't try to hide the little things that make you, you. Putting it all out there is scary, but it's the only way to connect with people on a real and personal level. If you are a closet geek, why hide it? If you hate something that people are calling "the next big thing," that's fine too! You don't have to hide who you are to succeed.

Making sure your heart and soul come through in your business is the best way for people to understand you, your products, and how you're different to your competitors. Keep this in mind when you write copy for your website and product descriptions—instead of trying to be someone you're not, use your own voice and watch your business shine.

HOW TO POSITION YOUR BRAND

Your brand positioning is where you fit into the market among your competitors. It also shows your customers that you are the right company for them based on their needs. In an overcrowded marketplace, it is essential to know where your business fits: knowing who you are and what you stand for can stop you being swayed by quick-fix sales techniques and jumping into things you otherwise wouldn't have.

Brand positioning is the process of positioning your brand in the mind of your customers. The idea is to identify and attempt to "own" a marketing niche for a brand, product, or service using various strategies including pricing, promotions, distribution, and packaging. The goal is to create a unique impression in the customer's mind so they associate your brand with something specific, desirable, and different from the competition.

WHY YOUR BRAND POSITION MATTERS

If you don't consider where your brand fits into the market, your customers will decide for you and it might not be where you want it to be. Are you looking to create a luxury brand or an everyday product? If it's luxury, then you don't want to come across as the cheaper option. Do you want your customers to feel happy, adored, valued, or pampered? Again, where you position your brand will determine how it is received.

Think about the expectations people have of your brand and how you deliver your services. Do you want to be seen as fashionable? Playful? Innovative? Stoic? Reliable? Ethical and eco-friendly? Define who you are and let this come across clearly in your design, content, and marketing platforms. Communicate this to your customers and everyone who comes into contact with your brand at every opportunity.

BRAND POSITIONING STRATEGY PROCESS

In order to create a position strategy, you must first identify your brand's uniqueness and determine what differentiates you from your competitors.

DETERMINE HOW YOUR BRAND IS CURRENTLY POSITIONING ITSELF

Look at every area where your brand comes into contact with potential customers. This might be your website, product range, promotional materials, pricing, brand identity, and social media conversations. Determine how your brand is currently positioned by asking what image these things portray? What is the story you are currently telling, and who is responding to your current market position? Where do you think you fit into the market for your industry. You might do this based on price or value. Are you expensive? Are you low priced? Do you offer a luxury service? Does your current brand communicate that?

Identify your direct competitors and understand how they position their brands.

Look to see where your competitors fall in the marketplace. Are they more or less expensive than you? Will your target market perceive them to be better than you? If so, why? What makes each of your competitors different? Are they all similar, in price, value, and image? Look for opportunities where you can dominate the market in a certain niche.

COMPARE YOUR POSITION TO YOUR COMPETITORS' TO IDENTIFY YOUR UNIQUENESS

What makes you different is how you will succeed in business. If you don't offer anything different to your more established competitors, then it will make it hard to try and gain loyal customers from them—why should someone buy from you instead?

DEVELOP A DISTINCT POSITION

Now that you have seen where your brand fits into the market, you will be able to see what opportunities there are to create a value-based positioning strategy. If all your competitors are offering high-end web-design services and no one is serving the lower end

for small business, non-profits, or educational establishments, you can use this opportunity to capture this position. It might sound sexier to say you are working on expansive projects, but if you can't compete with established companies with hundreds of employees you won't make money. Don't knock the potential of growing a thriving business based on serving smaller companies—after all, your aim is to become the "go-to" company for that niche, so go where the opportunity is.

WRITE A POSITIONING STATEMENT

Once you are clear about your brand's position, create a clear written description of what you do and for whom, including what is unique about you and where you fit into the market.

CREATING A BRAND PERSONALITY

Identifying and defining the identity and personality of your brand is crucial. Even if you don't actively define it, some sort of personality will come through, so it's best to think about it now, to make sure it's in line with the market position you are attempting to own. If you communicate conflicting messages to your target customers, you will seem distrustful and they won't want to work with you.

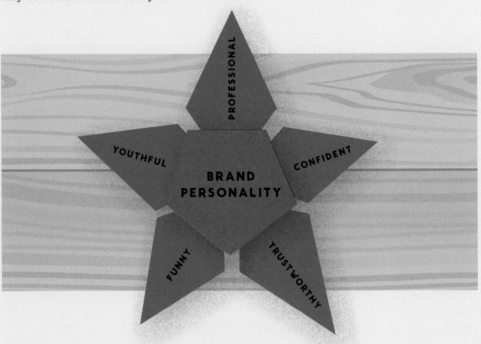

DEFINE YOUR BRAND PERSONALITY

A brand personality is a set of characteristics connected to a company or brand. These things shape how people feel about—and interact with—a company. Often, a brand's personality mirrors that of the target customer base because effective connections can be made that way.

Your brand personality doesn't necessarily have to be based on *your* personality—it's more important for your target customer to recognize themselves in your brand. They will respond to the way your brand communicates with them the same way they would a trusted friend so consider what character or personality type they would love. However, the personality needs to be an accurate reflection of your business vision, mission, values, promise, and purpose, or you will come across as inauthentic.

DO YOUR RESEARCH

Before you settle on a brand personality, do a little research. Know who you are, what you are selling, and who your customers are. Knowing where you fit into the market will help as well.

KNOW YOUR AUDIENCE

It's important to know who you'll be talking to and the likely reasons why your customers want to choose your brand over your competition. How do they want to communicate with you over social media? What are their likes and dislikes? Do they have any behavioral patterns that might impact on how you engage with them?

BRAINSTORM OPTIONS

What kind of voice would best relate to your core target market? How would your brand be described if it was a person? Ask yourself if your target customer respond to that voice?

NARROW IT DOWN

Once you have a few choices, you'll need to determine which personality type is the right fit. Consider your brand's story: how would you describe your product, website, or business to someone new?

CHOOSE BRAND TONE WORDS

Your brand personality is your brand's character. Some brands are fun and whimsical, and some are serious and straitlaced—what tone do you want your brand to convey? Choose three to five "tone words" that you can use consistently in all your brand designs and communications.

CREATE AND ESTABLISH THAT VOICE

You may find it helpful to find a visual image that represents your brand personality. If you are a young, playful brand is there a celebrity who fits this character? If you are a serious, determined brand maybe there is a business person in the public eye who exemplifies these attributes? When you are devising new product descriptions or communicating on social media, get their photo out or stick it somewhere visible. Pretend this person is writing the product description or sales page to their friend. How would they talk? What words would they use? How would they introduce themselves and make new friends? Keep their photo pinned to the wall to help you stay on point, and create a unique and consistent brand personality.

USE YOUR BRAND PERSONALITY TO GUIDE YOUR DESIGN

Once you determine your personality, it's time to start designing around it. What colors, typography, and imagery reflect your brand's personality? Be consistent in using the same style everywhere.

⑤

DEVELOPING YOUR BRAND EXPERIENCE

Your brand is embedded in all aspects of your business. If you create a unique and "wow-worthy" customer service experience, your customers will become loyal fans. Delivering a meaningful brand experience can help your customer connect with your company, so they return to use your services again and again. Give every customer the opportunity to become a raving fan by creating a brand experience to remember.

Developing your brand experience involves putting systems in place to wow your customer. You need to be consistent and deliver this experience to your customers with every interaction. If you go "off brand" they will lose faith in your company and take their money elsewhere.

As an example, take Innocent, the smoothie company. It is known for being a fun and

playful brand. It is evident on its packaging, its website, and even in its colorful (but natural) products. If the company started being rude to customers on social media, or changed its packaging to dull and dark colors, its customers would get confused. In this way, the brand experience would become diluted, the company would lose those things that make it different, and its customers would be more open to trying a competing brand.

WAYS YOU CAN CREATE AN EFFECTIVE BRAND EXPERIENCE

PUT THE CUSTOMER FIRST

When you create new products or services, create them for your customer. Don't develop based on what your industry or peers expect—put "real" people first. When you put the needs of real people at the forefront of developing your products, services, and marketing materials you create more meaningful experiences. Reflect the needs

and desires of your customers by adding value to their lives and not just creating for the sake of creating.

BE CONSISTENT WITH BRAND IMAGE

Your brand experience needs to be authentic to your brand. Your customers will come to expect a certain level of experience and tone with all interactions with your company and products. If you keep switching it up you will find it harder to build trust. It can be jarring as a consumer to believe something to be true about a company only for them to then try and become something else. If you are rebranding your company, be careful that you don't alienate your current customers. Keep your core values and brand promise the same, and grow your business based on an experience that your target customers respond to and value.

STORYTELLING

Everyone has a story—a reason they are at this point in their life, creating what they create. Whether you are an artist, designer, maker, seamstress, photographer, or sell vintage items, as creatives you have a passion for what you do and you need to share it. I believe people become connected through hearing each other's stories. Stories are powerful; they can draw us in and make us do things we never thought possible.

Consequently, marketing is no longer about icky practices—it's all about *connecting*.

The reality is people like to do business with people, and with the proliferation of online selling, consumers want to trust the business they are buying from. We can develop trust by showing who we are, being proud of what we do, and putting a face or a name to our work. We can engage through social media, develop a relationship, and provide honest insights into the people behind handmade goods and independent businesses.

SHARING YOUR PROCESS

Sharing your creative process is a great way to connect with your target audience. Much like telling your story, showing how you create can provide greater understanding about what you do and how you do it. It gives you the opportunity to show your customers how you get from your initial inspiration to the finished product, or why you have designed elements in a certain way. By nature, most of us are visual people, so actually showing your processes through photographs, video, or in person can be far more beneficial than just writing it down. This adds to your brand experience as you become known for including the customer in your journey.

CUSTOMER SERVICE

Getting and keeping customers is the cornerstone of your business—without people to buy your products and services, you won't have a business for long! Despite the importance of the customer and how you serve them, many business owners don't put a high importance on customer service, assuming that they deserve to win customers without even trying.

Long gone are the days of "once a customer, always a customer." People have a greater choice of where to shop and who to work with than ever before. It's also easier than ever for your customers to share their "treatment" online via social media with thousands of your potential customers. Poor feedback from just a few unsatisfied clients can cost you new clients in the future.

MAKE YOUR CUSTOMERS FEEL LOVED

LISTEN TO THEM

One of the best experiences a customer can have is to know they are understood, so always listen to your customers. Let them know you have heard them by rephrasing and communicating what they have told you. This makes sure that you and the customer are on the same page and lets customers know they've been heard.

USE YOUR MANNERS

Saying "please" and "thank you" is simply good manners, but not everyone remembers to do it. As a business owner, you must never forget—it is the quickest way to show your customer that you don't value them at all. Always be grateful to them, and demonstrate that by thanking them when they order from you or talk to you.

ALWAYS FOLLOW UP

If you get a customer inquiry or complaint, always follow up after it has been resolved. It adds a nice touch and makes your customer happy that you have taken the time to see how they are getting on. You can schedule reminders for follow-ups right in your inbox with most email providers. Also, if you say you are going to do something, always follow it through.

REMEMBER NAMES AND FACES

I worked in the employment industry years ago and my agency was competing for the best candidates with other local agencies. Without even realizing, I'd use a visual strategy to remember people's names for my own benefit, by remembering something about each person that was different. Maybe

they wore a red hat, came in with a child, rode a motorbike, or wore a colorful tie. This helped me to remember their face, name, and even their voice. They would phone up and (this was before caller ID!) I'd recognize who they were. They were always surprised that I remembered their name, and it meant they wanted to work with us over the competition. Everyone wants to feel like they matter. Using their name when you talk to them online or in person, and simply remembering who they are and what you spoke about before, is a surefire way to make someone feel valued.

SEND A HANDWRITTEN NOTE

Knowing that someone has taken time out of their day to write you a note makes anyone feel special. Send a short "thank you" note out with your orders, or when you send out your contracts. It adds personality and shows you care about building relationships, rather than just the transaction. Few people do this anymore, or they stop when they start getting too busy. Make it a priority, no matter how many orders you need to get out each day. Just a few words can put a smile on someone's face and help you stand out from your competitors who didn't bother.

GET FEEDBACK BY TALKING TO THEM

Customer feedback is invaluable, so whenever you have the opportunity to talk to your customers, take it. Ask them what you can do to improve your product or service. Ask them how they use your product. If you are at a craft fair, get instant feedback about the different scenarios where a customer might use your product. This can help you improve your selling pitch, marketing message, and product design. Even asking

about their day can make them feel special, while giving you helpful insights about how your customer uses your product or service.

MAKE THEM FEEL IMPORTANT

No one wants to feel they are just another order number. While meeting your sales goals might be the most important thing for you, if you pass that feeling on to your customers they won't be happy to shop with you again. Make your customer feel important by taking the time to listen, engage, and single them out for special treatment.

SHOW EMPATHY

Empathy is important in many aspects of your business. If you understand your customer, you can create better products and services for them; explain product benefits in a way they identify with, and connect with them on a deeper level.

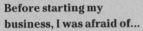

NESHA DESIGNS

WHO: Nesha Woolery
WHAT: Freelance graphic designer
WEBSITE: www.neshadesigns.com

Before starting my business, I was afraid of...
Being overwhelmed. I feared that the responsibility of running a one-woman business would be too much for me. What if I couldn't cope with the pressure? What if I wasn't experienced enough? What if I failed? These were all questions I battled with before starting my business and quitting my day job.

The one thing I wish I had known before starting my business...
Save enough money to live comfortably for six months.

I made some money from my new business, but not enough to keep my standard of living the same as it had been. If I'd saved a lot more before I quit my day job, I wouldn't have had to stress over paying my bills!

My best tip for new creative business owners...
Don't overthink. When you've just started your business, you want to get everything perfect before revealing it to the world, whether that is your new website, your pricing, or your blog... Nothing will ever be perfect and it will never feel truly ready, so just launch! Focus on making a profit—you can start perfecting things later.

My favorite thing about running my own business...
Freedom. When I was employed by someone else, it felt like there was a million boundaries. But now that I run my own business, I decide how many hours I work and how much money I make. The freedom is delicious!

6

MAKE IT
HAPPEN

DEVELOPING YOUR PRODUCT AND SERVICE OFFERINGS

Let's face it, the retail market is vastly overcrowded. It is easier than ever to start a website and reach customers all over the world, so consumers have a greater choice when it comes to deciding what they want to buy and who they want to work with. For product creators and designers it is no longer enough to make things just because you can. At least, not if you plan to sell them.

Lackluster products and services will be hard to sell because people simply won't want them. You might sell a few if the price is low enough, but you will struggle to build a long-term, sustainable business model.

So what can you do?

There is no magic formula for creating remarkable products. Your products need to offer something different, unique, and of great value to others. Competition is fierce and people are being more selective than ever with what they spend their money on. This is not only because of the dire global economy, but also because many people are choosing to buy less "stuff," to simplify their lives. The trend now is to focus on buying things that might cost a bit more, but are better made, higher quality, and longer lasting.

So what does this mean for product designers? Well, as Steve Jobs once said: "*If we keep putting great products in front of people, then they will open their wallets.*" It sounds crude, but it is true—people don't pay for mediocrity.

However, what makes a product great can differ from person to person, and it isn't just the tangible aspects of a product that affect that decision. So how do you create great products?

THINK AHEAD

What is your vision for the future? Where do you want to go with your business? If you know the bigger picture surrounding why you are in business, you will be able to focus on providing value and creating products that fit with this vision.

INNOVATE AND TAKE RISKS

Ask yourself how you can solve problems with your products and services. Innovate and be creative in finding these solutions. Instead of playing it safe, think about ways you can shake up your industry with a totally new product offering that is also answering a need and helping people flourish. Throw out the rule book and take risks!

LISTEN TO YOUR TARGET MARKET, BUT DON'T ALWAYS TAKE THEM LITERALLY

Monitor what your target market is saying by keeping your ear to the ground, listening, and joining in conversations. Read articles, blogs, newspapers, Tweets, Facebook statuses, and talk to people at craft fairs—anything that

gets you closer to discovering what your target market really needs.

Find out what your audience thinks it wants, then use this information to build a better product. Remember, not everyone knows what they *really* want, especially as they may not be aware of the full range of possibilities. As Henry Ford said: "*If I had asked people what they wanted, they would have said faster horses.*" So listen, but interpret the real need. If people want a faster horse, provide something faster, but don't limit yourself to thinking it has to be a horse.

THINK OUTSIDE THE BOX

With easy access to inspiration online, through blogs and websites such as Pinterest, design and products are starting to feel homogenized.

When everyone is drawing from the same inspiration pool it makes sense that the work we create will start to look similar. Counteract this by finding inspiration in less obvious places. Limit how much time you spend browsing online inspiration sources while you are in the initial product development phase, and be creative in your approach to new product ideas.

PRODUCT TESTING

When you think you have your final product, test it with people who you think want and need it. Send them a copy or give them a sample, and ask them what they think. Don't prompt too much, instead listen to their opinion and suggestions. This can help you tweak a good idea and turn it into a great one.

HOW TO ACCURATELY PRICE PRODUCTS AND SERVICES

There are two main aspects to pricing for your business. The first is to get an accurate idea of what your product or service costs you to make or provide. The second is your overall pricing strategy, which impacts customer perceptions and positions your brand in the marketplace.

Pricing needs to be at a sustainable level. Undersell what your products are worth and you will struggle to bring in enough revenue to grow your business long term.

START OUT RIGHT

Develop a pricing system so you can be consistent, and use a strategy to build out your product range.

PRODUCT PRICING FORMULA

The formula below is a great starting point if you are unsure how to price your products, as the profit is built in from the beginning.

BREAKING IT DOWN

The first section of the formula is your break-even price. This price helps you to see how much your products need to make at a minimum level, especially if you plan to wholesale now or in the future. It includes:

MATERIALS

Work out how much each product costs you to make in terms of materials, such as fabric, paint, canvas, wood, thread, and so on. Also include less obvious material costs such as packaging and "thank you" notecards to be sent out with each order.

LABOR COSTS

Your labor costs are how much it costs someone (you, an employee, or contractor) to make the product. Remember, you will only spend a certain number of hours creating—

the rest of the time will be marketing, doing social media, packaging orders, updating your website, and trips to the post office. So set an hourly rate that covers those tasks too. It's tempting to set a low hourly rate, but it needs to be realistic and sustainable. How much would you have to pay someone else to do the same tasks? Start from the minimum wage and work your way up depending on your skill set, experience, and all the different tasks that need to be done to get your product to market.

EXPENSES

These are your overhead costs, which include things like electricity, studio rental fees, Paypal fees, office supplies, and all the other essential outgoing costs that you need to run your business.

HOW TO WRITE WEB COPY

Before you jump into designing your website, start planning out your web copy. It can be hard to write to fit a pre-designed space, but if you've written your copy in advance you'll be able to design the pages with the space you need. Your content and design need to work together seamlessly to attract your ideal client. What you say and write on your website will be the clincher between whether you get a sale or not, so patchy copy, or something you wrote as an afterthought to fit into a limited space, doesn't make good business sense.

The best web copy is user-focused, clear, and to the point. It also needs to be persuasive to help you achieve your marketing and business goals.

KNOW YOUR PURPOSE

It doesn't matter if you are writing a blog post or a web page, each piece of copy needs a clear point. Determine it before you start writing. Ask yourself what the copy is for? What are you trying to achieve with this piece of writing?

IT'S NOT ABOUT YOU

For your web copy to work, you need to put your customers first. Know who you are writing for and what they respond to. That way, you can make sure you write copy that attracts them.

In order to persuade the reader that your product/business is right for them, you need to put them at the heart of everything you write. Your customers probably don't care how many awards you have won or whether you like chocolate or not. What they do want to know is what you can do for them.

Write about the benefits of your product or service rather than the features. Tell them how the product will help them or save them money.

KEEP IT SIMPLE

When potential customers visit your website they want to be able to scan your page and quickly find the information they need to make a decision about whether they will choose your company over another.

As a rule, make sure you don't use technical language or industry jargon that they might not understand.

Keep your copy to the point, with short paragraphs and headings to break up large amounts of text.

Clarity is more important than trying to be clever and ending up being misunderstood. To be effective, get to the core of the message you want to share.

USE YOUR VOICE

People like to do business with people. By using your own voice and adding stories or personal examples, you can make a deeper connection with your readers. Be conversational. Write as though you are talking to your ideal customer and you will find that you will connect authentically with your target audience. It also helps to differentiate you from all your competitors— it is what makes you, YOU. Trying to copy someone else's style won't work.

WRITE NATURALLY

Your web copy needs to sound natural for your target market to respond. Allow them to learn who you are before they work with you. Stilted, marketing speak sounds false and doesn't connect very well.

CALL TO ACTION

What do you want people to do? Make sure you ask them. Every piece of writing for your website should include a call to action—an instruction for what to do next. Do you want them to contact you? To buy? To share your blog post with their social media followers? Make it clear what you want, and make it easy for them to follow through.

BE AWARE OF SEO, BUT DON'T BE A SLAVE TO IT

SEO (Search Engine Optimization) refers to making your website easier to find for the search engines. That way, when people look online for a solution to their problem, your website will be one of the options that come up first.

I don't believe in forcing SEO. Natural and organic optimization is much better. You can't outsmart the search engines, so don't try. Instead they will penalize your site if you use untoward tactics.

If you do want to be more intentional by using targeted keywords, don't force them into your copy. Instead, choose a few phrases that you want to highlight and use them where it makes sense. You can put them in your headings, subheadings, and service and product descriptions.

You'll have more success if you use different terms and words to say the phrase you want to rank for. It also sounds more natural.

6

HOW TO GET A WEBSITE

Whatever your business, having a website is essential. Even if you are only selling offline at galleries or craft fairs, every creative entrepreneur needs a website to attract new business, supply information to customers, and show their work. If you are selling online—even if it is via a marketplace like Etsy—you still need your own website to direct people to.

If you don't have a domain name yet for your business, get it now. For just a few dollars per year you can ensure that when the time comes to create your website, no one else has the name you want. Even if you don't need a full website now, you can forward your domain to a marketplace shop or have a simple place-holding page containing your contact details. Just make sure you buy the domain name for your business before someone else does.

GETTING STARTED

1) CHOOSE A DOMAIN NAME

When you choose your domain name, the following points will help you get it right:

- Go with a .com (if possible) as it is the traditional "global" tag.
- Choose a domain name that is as close to your business name as possible.
- Make it easy to say and spell.
- Don't include hyphens or numbers.
- If you're not sure what to choose, use your own name.
- If the domain you want isn't available, be creative and add or shorten the words.

2) GET WEB HOSTING

In order for your website to be seen online, you also need to have web hosting. This is where your files, content, and photos will be stored. You have two main options here:

you either host the files yourself, through a web-hosting company such as GoDaddy or Bluehost, or you use a third party, such as Squarespace, that will host your files for you. You can pay for hosting upfront for a year, but many companies will give you the option to pay monthly.

DO IT YOURSELF

Once you have your domain name and your web hosting, you can create a website. One of the best options when you're starting out is to create your website yourself. This can look just as professional as an expensive website, and can draw in customers just as effectively.

If you want to be able to tinker with the design a lot, then a content management system (CMS) such as Wordpress, along with a premium theme might be the best option. Although free themes are available, these usually have design restrictions. They are also used more widely, so your website could end up looking like a competitor's. When you buy a premium theme, you can often tweak it to make it look how you want it to.

If you simply want to drop your content into a pre-existing template, then Squarespace is a good option. You pay monthly for the service, but it is easy to have a beautiful, professional-looking website up and running in just a few minutes. You can also tweak the templates to make them fit your brand, although there is less flexibility than Wordpress.

E-COMMERCE OPTIONS

If you will be selling your goods or services online then you need an e-commerce solution. Shopify is by far the best solution out there for small businesses right now. It has different price levels depending on your needs and will also host your files so you are paying for that too. You can use a simple "out of the box" theme or get a designer to create a custom one for you.

Squarespace also has an e-commerce capability, or you can use Big Cartel. Big Cartel is different in that it doesn't host all your files. It is also less flexible, but if you find a suitable premium theme you can get started quickly. Big Cartel is easy to set up and add products to, so if you are looking for a simple solution it is a good option.

MARKETPLACE SITES

Marketplace sites are good for very small, starter businesses that want everything taken care of. Etsy is the most popular, and for a small listing fee you can upload as many products as you want. When you make a sale, a small percentage is deducted as commission, and you get the balance. One of the main benefits of Etsy for new businesses is that it has a high volume of traffic—people primed and ready to buy.

There are some downsides, though. Because the site is so large, you are competing with a lot of other sellers, so you need to optimize your listings and product descriptions to be found through searches. You can also drive traffic directly to your shop, but there is no guarantee that a prospective purchaser won't look at your competitors as well. You are also limited with design options.

After a few years selling on Etsy, many sellers graduate to their own website.

WORKING WITH A DESIGNER OR WEB DEVELOPER

If you don't have web design knowledge, then you might want to work with a designer or web developer to get your site up and running. A web designer will normally only work on the look of your site, then pass the files to a developer for them to build it. The price of this varies depending on if you go with a freelancer or larger web design studio. The more complicated the design, or the more custom elements you have, the higher the price will be.

Make sure you are able to update the site yourself so you can add photos, edit text, and blog without needing to get your web designer to help each time.

NIKKI McWILLIAMS

WHO: Nikki McWilliams
WHAT: Biscuit-inspired homewares
WEBSITE: www.nikkimcwilliams.com

Before starting my business, I was afraid of...

When I started my business, I don't remember feeling afraid. I was still working part time (in a retail "day job" that I knew I didn't want to do forever), so the time I was able to spend working on my business was a welcome departure from this.

However, when the time came for me to become 100% self-employed, I was terrified! I was worried that I wouldn't make enough money to support myself. I thought that I could be being foolish and a bit self-indulgent in leaving a well-paid job to "follow my dreams."

That was five years ago, and I've never looked back!

The one thing I wish I had known before starting my business...

How to do a tax return—the first one was stressful!

My best tip for new creative business owners...

Work hard, stay focused, and remember to rest as well—downtime is important.

My favorite thing about running my own business...

Being able to make my own hours. When I worked my "day job" I missed almost every family celebration for almost four years! I love running my own business, but having the freedom to have a social life and spend time with family and friends is so important to me.

POSITIONING YOURSELF AS AN EXPERT

⑥

Being seen as an expert in your field is essential if you are offering a service as a designer, business coach, or consultant, but it can also benefit product makers. This is because everyone wants to work with or buy from a credible company with the reputation of being an expert in their industry.

Imagine being the go-to company for the media whenever they want to talk about your industry. Maybe you sell healthy snacks for children and the media need someone to discuss healthy eating options for children on their TV show. If you were on TV talking about your children's snacks, viewers would see you as an expert—why would you be there if you didn't know what you were talking about?

Being featured in this way establishes credibility, trust, and authority over other brands and companies. It also allows you to put a link to the interview on your website or blog, share it on social media, and add "as featured on" to your product descriptions.

HOW DO YOU DEFINE AN EXPERT?

The widely known definition of an expert is someone that knows their area of expertise better than anyone else in their field. You might be worried that this doesn't apply for you (especially if you are just starting out), but you can still be considered an expert if you simply know more than others on a certain topic.

For example, you might know more about healthy eating options for children than the average parent, which is enough to teach and inform those with less knowledge than you. If you get featured in press, media, and on popular blogs, you will be seen as an expert.

Even if there are other people who have more knowledge than you, if your target market isn't aware of them, then they won't be seen as experts.

No matter where you are in your field at the moment, continued learning about what is happening in your industry is essential to being considered an expert. So keep learning and stay informed about your subject matter. As you get started with promoting yourself, and showing off your expertise, remember that it may take some time for you to become better known. However, employing the following tactics will help extend your reach.

HOW TO BE SEEN AS AN EXPERT

EXPERT INTERVIEWS

Journalists are always looking for experts to include in their stories. Make a list of different publications and blogs that use quotes from experts or feature experts and then research how you can pitch yourself to them. It's not just journalists and bloggers who could use you as an expert source—local news shows, newspapers, magazines, and morning TV segments also need them, so let them know you are willing to be called upon if and when they need someone.

GUEST POSTS

Guest posting on other people's websites can help establish you as an expert. Many sites allow guest writers, so look for those that accept submissions. Research the type of content they normally post and come up with some ideas that would be a relevant fit for their readers or viewers.

SPEAKING ENGAGEMENTS

Getting up on stage in front of a room full of people is another way you can present yourself as an authority in your field. It might sound scary, but you can start small; local events and talks in schools or for small businesses can help build your confidence and experience. Craft one or two signature talks that you can become known for. Once you've gained experience at smaller events you can seek out larger, national events.

EDITORIAL FEATURES

Being seen in national magazines is one of the best ways of establishing credibility with your target customers. Devise a PR strategy and work on building relationships with magazine editors and columnists who may be able to include your products in roundups. Maximize any press you receive by sharing it on social media, to your email list, and by having it visible on your website.

SOCIAL MEDIA

You can use social media to interact with your target customers, but it's not just a way of sharing your work. You can also use it to share your expertise. Consider the different ways that you can share your knowledge as an expert by engaging further: answer questions, host Q+A chats, and let people get to know you as the expert in your subject.

CREATING
A LOOKBOOK

Lookbooks are just that: books that show off your brand's "look." They were traditionally used by fashion businesses, but more and more product businesses are branching out and using them to help sell their products. Lookbooks are a great way to position your brand in the market and they can help people visualize how the item will fit into their homes or life.

Lookbooks feature high-quality lifestyle photography and often use models to show how the products will look in real life. They can be printed and sent to retailers and press, but nowadays many are displayed online or distributed digitally.

Lookbooks can often be confused with catalogs. The main difference is that a catalog will have direct product shots, prices, and product information for people to order from. A lookbook is about creating an atmosphere or showing the "look" of the item in its natural setting. The aim is to create aspirational lifestyle images that your target market wants to be a part of.

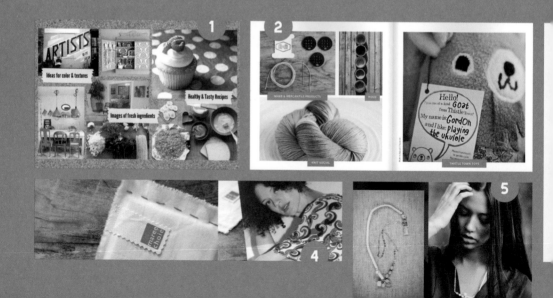

PLANNING YOUR LOOKBOOK

CONSIDER YOUR TARGET MARKET

What do they look like, what images do they respond to? If you're going to use a model, make it someone that your target market can relate to while still being aspirational. When deciding on location options consider places that your target market might visit, or an apartment/home/garden they can see themselves living in.

CREATE A MOODBOARD

Decide which products you want to include and how you want to portray them. Action shots with models are a great way to show energy, youth, and excitement. You can create a vision board or Pinterest board showing ideas and different shots. These can then be turned into a storyboard that you can work with at the photoshoot.

PHOTOGRAPHER VS. DIY

If you have the budget, then book a professional photographer who understands the vision you have for the lookbook. If you are short on funds, you can take the photos yourself; just keep it simple, clear, and bright, with not too much going on in each shot.

PROPS AND LOCATIONS

Gather items that will work well with your collection. Aim for complementary items that don't steal the limelight from your own products. When scouting for locations, make sure you consider the atmosphere you want to create. Parks, fairgrounds, the beach, or woodland each create a different feel. Just be sure to check with your local authority in case you need a license to shoot there.

1. A moodboard for a new range of food products. It includes lifestyle images, and other objects that reflect the products' color and typographic style.

2/3. Digital lookbook for Get Crafty. It also includes shots of the studio, plus interviews with the makers.

4. Maree Choi's lookbook for a new printed fashion range is delivered with a handmade pouch that gives it an additional feeling of value.

5. Craft and Culture jewelry. This beautifully produced lookbook shows products shot against natural backgrounds. Sepia-toned photography of the models gives an expensive and authentic look to the range.

6. Wedding accessories moodboard.

SETTING YOUR BRAND APART WITH PHOTOGRAPHY

6

One of the biggest difficulties when trying to sell your products online is getting perfect product photos. It can be hard to achieve a professional look that will represent your work in the best light, but it's really important to try and get the best photos you can. After all, it's often the only opportunity your customers have to see your work before they buy. Develop your own style of photography and use it consistently to enhance your brand story.

FIND YOUR OWN STYLE TO STAND OUT FROM COMPETITORS

Look at what your competitors are doing. Then do the opposite. Most industries use the same style of photo or the same props. Organic companies use brown kraft paper for packaging, soap companies use flowers and herbs to show how natural they are, designers present their past work in photos of Apple computers—it's monotonous and

makes all these companies blend in. Take a risk and do something different. Doing something out of the ordinary will not only make a statement, but mean that you will also be one step ahead of the competition, simply because you will be remembered!

REVISIT YOUR BRAND VALUES

Use your brand values and tone words to help you choose which props to use. The props will help tell a story and add a feel to your photographs. Make sure this feeling is in line with your brand. Ensure your photos and packaging are not just pretty, but add to the brand and product story in some way.

DEVELOP A PHOTO STYLING COLOR PALETTE

Taking inspiration from your brand color palette, develop a photo styling palette that you can use to keep your photos consistent. Selecting props and backgrounds can be daunting, but limiting your color palette is a simple way to give your photographs a cohesive feel.

LOOK FOR ITEMS YOU MAY ALREADY HAVE AROUND THE HOUSE TO ENHANCE YOUR PHOTOS

What can you use that you already have? Consider everyday household objects, small toys, or even drawing or painting your photo backgrounds. Add things that are personal to you in similar or contrasting colors to your styling palette. Different shades of the same color work extremely well. Props don't have to be expensive—even if you can't find anything suitable at home, you can try thrift stores or found objects like leaves or wild flowers. Remember that "less is more" and choose your items carefully. All you need

are a few things to enhance and complement your products.

RECREATE THE LIFESTYLE SETTING

What type of products are you selling? Choose props to help you recreate the scene your products will be used in. The purpose of styling a shoot is to show your potential customers your products in a way they can visualize using them. If you sell party decorations, show these in a party setting. Make cushions? Show them on a sofa as part of a living room's decor. How would your products look in use in your customers home? Recreate that look so they can easily imagine how your item would fit into their life and home.

CHOOSE LOCATION CAREFULLY

Where you take your photos is important. Your background needs to fit with your brand. If your business is rustic and natural, use a similarly fitting background. If your style is more clean lines and modern, work with an all-white background and modern shapes. Keep background noise to a minimum and stay true to your design style and the purpose of your products.

BE CONSISTENT

Once you have defined your brand photo style, use it everywhere, from social media to your website. Be consistent, so your customers recognize your brand immediately. If you switch it up too often, you will confuse your target audience.

PROMOTE
YOUR WORK

WHAT MARKETING AND PR CAN DO FOR YOU

Many small business owners are not clear on the differences between marketing, PR (Public Relations), and advertising. All three are a form of promotion, but they achieve different things, in different ways.

WHAT IS MARKETING?

Marketing focuses on determining what your customers need and want, so you are able to profitably create products and services that they will buy. It involves communicating value to your customers and balancing that with making a profit. Marketing is essential to all businesses, because without knowing who your customers are and what your business offers, you will find it hard to sell.

MARKETING FOCUSES ON PEOPLE

Building communities and relationships with like-minded people can make great things happen. It's people who buy things and it's people who sell things. All your customers want to know is that you understand their needs as a person. There are a few ways you can do this:

- If you have a decent product or service and a clear target market, just talk to them. Communicate in any way you know how.
- If you can create great content that connects with your target market you will start to build a community of people interested in what you do.
- If you can talk openly and passionately about things you and others are interested in, those people will be inspired.
- If you can be helpful, personable, honest, and real, the word will spread and more people will buy your products.

Marketing has not changed much over the years, but the way we reach people has. Social media has allowed us to talk and connect with more people than ever before, so use it to help grow your business.

WHAT IS PR?

Firstly, PR is not the same as advertising. With advertising, you pay for space in a magazine, a blog, or directory, for example, with the hope that someone (or lots of people) will follow through to your website/shop/blog to buy your products. In contrast, most forms of PR are free—it costs nothing but your time and can have great results if done correctly.

PR is all about raising awareness of your brand. Without it, no one will know your business exists. PR puts your business in front of the people you want to know about it, for free. There are numerous ways to do this, including pitching to blogs and magazines, writing guest blog posts, blogging, and using social media. All of these things allow you to reach people and influence perceptions of your brand.

However, it may or may not increase sales immediately; it is a long-term strategy. You are building relationships and laying the groundwork so that when someone wants your product, they remember you.

PR can be beneficial to your business because consumers want to know who they are buying from. A combination of public relations and social media can help position you in the market, connect with your target audience, and build trust. Being seen on the best blogs and magazines for your industry can not only increase sales, but it can also get you noticed among industry insiders who can provide exciting opportunities and collaborations.

PR has similar benefits to word of mouth, but on a larger scale. Instead of a handful of friends telling friends about a business, you have respected bloggers, magazine editors, and journalists telling their readers how great you are. You can't beat that kind of coverage!

THE IMPORTANCE OF STORYTELLING

Telling stories is the basis of how you will communicate and engage with your target customer. When you tell your story, it reveals who you are and the values that guide you. Storytelling is a powerful way to connect with others, because people like to build relationships with companies that make them feel something, and that they feel a connection to. When they buy products it's because they resonate with the story being told.

Today, the marketplace is so large and the competition so great that you need to find ways of getting noticed. It is very important to know who your potential customers are and to make sure your product is something that fulfills their needs, but even then you may have created a product that fills the same need or has the same benefits as hundreds—if not thousands—of others. So how are you going to stand out?

The answer is through your story.

For your story to have impact, it has to be truthful. It also needs to connect to a larger shared value or experience. When we hear stories about underdogs that finally make it, we understand. It taps into something we hope for ourselves. It is a story that is told over and over again in movies, novels, and in advertising because it works. People respond to it.

It also works in business. With the proliferation of online selling, consumers need to trust who they are buying from. You can develop trust by showing who you are, being proud of yourself, and putting a face or a name to your work. You can engage through social media, develop a relationship, and provide real, honest insights into the people behind creative products and services.

CRAFTING YOUR STORY

KNOW YOUR AUDIENCE

The more time you spend understanding your customers and the people you are trying to sell to, the better equipped you will be when it comes to crafting a story they resonate with. This has an impact on all aspects of your business.

BE TRUTHFUL

Look at the pertinent details of your journey to this point. What stands out? What adds to the narrative? If you are a health coach, was there a time in your life when you weren't healthy? When did you turn your life around? If you've always been healthy, what was it that made you want to change the lives of others through your work? Opening up about your past and adding real memories that evoke emotion will make you more relatable.

LOOK TO LESSONS YOU HAVE LEARNED ON YOUR JOURNEY SO FAR

Everyone has a story, and there is a reason you are at this point in your life, creating what you create. Whether you are an artist, designer, maker, seamstress, photographer, or you sell vintage items, as a creative you have a passion for what you do and you need to share it. People connect through hearing other people's stories. Stories are powerful, they can draw us in and inspire us to do amazing things.

TELLING THE CUSTOMER'S STORY

Telling the customer's story instead of your own can also work in marketing. This works well for products or services where there is a clear customer pain point. You can use storytelling to show what their life is like without your offering. Pinpoint the emotion behind the pain and make them understand how their life can be improved once they buy what you're selling.

SHARING YOUR CREATIVE PROCESS

Sharing your process is another great way to connect with your target audience. Showing how you create can provide greater understanding about what you do and how you do it. It gives you the opportunity to show how you get from your initial inspiration to the finished product, or why you have designed elements in a certain way.

By nature, most of us are visual people so actually showing your process—through photos, video, or in person—can be far more beneficial than just writing it down. The aim is to give an overview of how you work, so you can inform and engage your audience, and connect on a deeper level than them just viewing finished products in your shop.

⑦

REFINE YOUR COMPANY NARRATIVE AND DEVELOP YOUR ELEVATOR PITCH

Many creative entrepreneurs struggle when talking about their business. It's hard to feel inspired or compelled to buy when the person trying to convince you doesn't have any confidence in what they do. To make sure you're able to sell yourself and your company confidently, you need to craft a compelling company narrative and an "elevator pitch" that can be easily adapted according to your audience. This narrative should grab the attention of whoever you are telling it to—your aim is to make them sit up and take notice through engaging conversation. Your company narrative should explain why they should care about your products or business in the first place.

IDENTIFY YOUR AUDIENCE

Defining your target audience for your pitch is the first step to being able to write a message that they will connect with. Are you starting a conversation with potential customers about what you do? Are you trying to pitch for investment? Or do you simply want a few lines to be able to explain what you do to family and friends? Tailor your pitch to who you anticipate you'll be telling it to.

EXPLAIN WHAT YOU DO AND WHO YOU DO IT FOR

Make it clear from the start who you are targeting with your business. A business coach might say "I teach busy yoga teachers how to supplement their income through digital products." An artist might say "I create large custom canvas art for office spaces." This one line needs to be compelling enough to keep your audience's attention. Think about ways in which you can make it sound interesting to the person listening. The words you choose can make a big difference. What if instead of "supplement their income" you used "make more money?" What about

changing "make some extra cash" to "triple your income?" Each phrase will have a different effect, so use the one that will have the most impact on the person listening.

SHOW HOW YOU ARE DIFFERENT FROM THE COMPETITION

Once you have shown what you do and who for, it's time to convince them why your product is better than all the other choices out there that fill that same need or provide similar benefits. Why *your* business coaching? What is your USP (unique selling point)? Maybe your coaching is different because it's in short ten-minute increments so your yoga customers can fit it in easily around their busy lives? Why your canvas art? You could explain that you produce fully customized art based on branded colors. Find that thing that makes your product or service different, then add that to your message.

ASK A QUESTION

Asking questions helps to engage your audience. However, ensure these are open-ended questions that can't be answered with

a straight "yes" or "no." Bring your audience into the conversation. For example, if you are pitching for a new coaching client, you might ask "how could your life be different if you doubled your income?" It allows them to put themselves in the position of how your service can change them and their lives, and gives you the opportunity to keep talking. You can then answer any questions confidently, because you have their attention and you know you can help them.

PUT IT TOGETHER

When you have completed each section of your pitch, it's time to put it together so that it sounds natural. It shouldn't be too long—the idea is that you are on a quick elevator ride with your ideal client—so you should be able to pitch what you do, and why and how you do it, in less than a minute. Ideally, your pitch should be around 30 seconds. You want to be able to succinctly say what they need to hear, then end with a question to keep the conversation going.

Once you have crafted a narrative that encompasses all these elements it's time to use it! You can also incorporate this as a marketing message in your promotional activities, such as your bios on social media networking sites, your advertising slogan, your website copy, and your packaging. Monitor the reaction to your message to see if the right people understand it. When your marketing message is on point, you'll notice an increase in sales. This means you are connecting on a deeper level with the potential customers who are most likely to buy your product.

DEFINING YOUR TARGET MARKET

Everyone in business has heard the term "target market." It's one of those headings on a business or marketing plan that as creatives we rush to with a sigh of relief. Defining your target market sounds straightforward; yet when they are asked who they are targeting, so many business owners say something so broad they might as well have said "everyone."

As a small business you need a niche—a segment or section of society that your product is perfect for. Marketing to everyone may be OK for national companies who have the budget to reach everyone, but as an independent business you need your clients to be passionate enough about your products that they buy them. You want your customers to be ambassadors who spread the word, and they will only do that if you manage to connect with them as individuals.

So, who are you targeting? Who is your ideal client—the person who will buy your products all of the time? Who are they, no really, *who*? You need to know exactly who your ideal customer is. Think of one person. Try to visualize them. If you are a women's jewelery designer, who is the ideal woman you are creating your products for? She wears your jewelery, but what else does she wear? What clothes does she wear to work—is she classic or casual? Does she wear the same jewelery to parties as she does to the office, or does she try to change her look? You should be clear on this before you dive deeper into defining your target market for marketing purposes.

USING ONLINE TOOLS TO FIND YOUR TARGET MARKET

Once you have a better idea of who your target customer is, it's time to track them down. These days there is a host of online tools available to help you find them, some of which are free and others that you need to pay for. These tools help you pinpoint where your target market is, where those people are hanging out, and what terms they are searching for. This information is invaluable when it's time to start targeting them.

KEYWORD SEARCH

Identifying the right keywords is imperative in target marketing. It is these words that indicate what it is people are looking for and whether they will want to buy your product.

Google has a number of options for searching keywords that your target customer may be using. Google Insights for Search is a free service that allows you to simply type in a few words related to your goods. It shows you how much interest there is in a particular word or phrase and can give you an idea of buzz words you can use later to generate interest from the right people. Start off searching for phrases that came up when identifying your target customer. Next, search for phrases for your products or processes you use.

Google also has another keyword tool related to its AdWords service. This keyword generator is a great way to track which words are at the top of your target market's searches and can help you develop your marketing strategy.

Once you know the words your target customers are using to find similar products through search engines, you can start to delve a bit deeper. Using Google Analytics, the code embedded in your website can provide precious information to find your target market. Google Analytics records which country someone is viewing your website from, which site they were using before they came to yours, the search terms they used to end up on your page, and even which browser they used. All of this information should help you become more efficient in your marketing efforts.

START TARGETING

It is a lot easier to sell to someone when you know a lot about them. For a start, it makes it easier to buy advertising if you know which

blogs your target market reads. You can run searches on Twitter to look for those keywords you identified earlier, and then you can begin to add content and value to your website that is rich in the information your target market is looking for.

Get to know your customer and encourage them to get to know you via Twitter and Facebook. Your keyword search will have highlighted the trigger words that will help you find them on other websites and group pages. Read their blogs, comment on their posts, and build relationships. Then your customers will champion your brand and you personally. You will not only build friendships and a community for your business, but you will also develop a deeper understanding of who your customer is and what they are looking for.

HOW TO CONNECT AND ENGAGE WITH PEOPLE

Marketers like to talk a lot about "connecting" and "engaging" with people, and that's for one simple reason: it works. Your business can't exist in a vacuum. You need to reach out to others, be vulnerable, and open to building new relationships. These relationships become a network of people on your side, fighting for your success. Whether it's a repeat customer or the delivery man, they all impact your business.

When we talk about engaging with customers, we mean keeping them interested in who you are and what you are selling. You do this through conversation and being there to listen to what they have to say, regardless of whether it's a concern or praise.

We often talk about having conversations and engaging customer service as if they are new concepts. Of course, they're not new—they have been around for years. With the advent of social media platforms, such as Twitter and Facebook, the tools for having these conversations and sharing your work has changed, but the reasons for doing so have stayed the same: people want to feel connected to what they buy and the people they buy from.

The ultimate aim for increasing engagement is to build relationships. After all, if you have one million social media followers, but no one replies or engages with you, then what is the point? Vanity metrics don't make a business succeed, but relationships with interested people can help you sell more.

INCREASING ENGAGEMENT

You will naturally connect and engage with people while doing business, but you might struggle to increase that engagement and develop the relationship further. If you want to grow your audience naturally, ask and encourage them to contribute, then thank them when they do—you will find your audience will start engaging with you more.

BE YOURSELF

If you want to connect meaningfully with others, you need to be yourself. People can sense if you are putting on an act or trying to be something you're not. Be genuine and people will feel more comfortable interacting with you. Decide what it is you stand for and stick to it. Refer back to your core values. Don't be swayed by what other people are doing or telling you you should do to become a success. We're all different, and being original and following your own path is the best way to encourage the right people to connect with you.

LET IT HAPPEN ORGANICALLY

Grow your social media followers and blog audience by posting relevant content, not by forcing or begging. Audiences are more engaged when they find you, like what they see or read, and are able to decide for themselves whether they want to get involved further or not. Gimmicks and contests may increase your audience quickly, but they won't care about what you have to say or sell, so are less likely to engage.

CUSTOMER EXPERIENCE

Turn every contact into a memorable experience. People are often looking for more than a basic transaction. People remember when an experience is pleasurable or ghastly. Make it the former by being friendly, approachable, and doing something unexpected. Remember your customer's name and use it when emailing, talking on the phone, or on social networks. Offer a personalized service and custom options, and remember past interactions and orders. People will be more willing to engage with you if you show that you value them.

ALWAYS SAY THANK YOU

One of the best ways to encourage people to engage more is to say "thank you" when they do it. It shows that you value them taking the time to join in the conversation and it also helps encourage others to do the same because they will see that you are actively engaged with your audience.

ASK YOUR AUDIENCE TO ENGAGE WITH YOU

Some people don't respond to hints or suggestions at all. If you want someone to do something specific, spell it out! Ask your audience to engage with you. Subtle hints or hoping for interaction is not going to work. People don't want to misread situations, so unless you are specific they won't try to second guess what you want them to do. Instead, they will just carry on with their day. If you ask for their opinion, or ask them to join in and add to the conversation, then they are more likely to do so.

MONITOR AND ASSESS WHAT'S WORKING

In order to know what works best you should monitor the results and assess what's working and what isn't. If you try a new method or technique, keep an eye on how many people respond. This is easy to do using social media. With Twitter, see how many @ mentions you get to a question, Tweet, or link. You can also check how many people have Retweeted you.

On your blog, you can look out for comments and also use Google Analytics and Pinterest to determine who is sharing your blog posts. Sometimes a blog post that initially seems like it received little in the way of comments, has been shared hundreds of times and has been commented on elsewhere. It's also very insightful to see referrals from sites that mention you and you can build a relationship with the bloggers that like what you post.

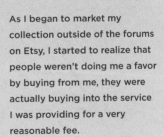

ONETENZEROSEVEN

WHO: Sophie Howarth
WHAT: Jewelry designer
WEBSITE: www.onetenzeroseven.com

Thoughts on pricing your products...

My prices started out as figures plucked from thin air, and the more I didn't sell my products, the less I believed in them. The first few sales felt like my friends on Etsy were doing me a favor by buying from me, and I constantly worried that I was charging too much, when in fact I was charging very little for the work I put in.

Those initial months were spent between tearing my hair out and soaking up every piece of advice I could possibly squeeze out of people. I learned that I needed to give potential customers a reason to buy from me instead of someone else.

As I began to market my collection outside of the forums on Etsy, I started to realize that people weren't doing me a favor by buying from me, they were actually buying into the service I was providing for a very reasonable fee.

As my prices increased, I sold more and more. It was surreal, but the lack of sales in those early days was just a rite of passage for a start-up. These days I charge more than ever, I'm self-employed, and my business is flourishing.

PRESS AND MEDIA KITS

⑦

Whether you are an artist, blogger, designer, crafter, or vintage seller, there will come a time when you want to get more awareness of your business in the media. Instead of waiting for the media to find you, contact them yourself with a press kit.

Press kits (or "media kits," as they are sometimes called), are information packets that you can send out to prospective media to inform them of your business. If you are thinking of approaching the press—in particular, magazines or newspapers—you will want to send them some information about you and your company so you can get their attention.

Press kits can be sent out in a digital format or you can create a physical kit. Most media outlets will expect to receive a digital kit, as they are easy to email over, don't take up much space, and are also kind to the environment. Physical kits still have a place, though—if you are sending out samples to TV shows, national magazines, or potential stockists it makes more sense to send a physical press kit with it.

You can send your press kit out to reporters, journalists, magazine editors, bloggers, and TV shows. These are busy people, so you want to make it easy for them to write about you by supplying all the information they might need to put a story together.

You can also use your press kit as a marketing tool to send to potential sponsors or advertisers. Many bloggers have press kits that feature information aimed at getting an advertiser's attention such as reader demographics, traffic stats, sponsor rates, and ad sizes.

THINGS TO INCLUDE IN YOUR PRESS KIT

It's important to appreciate that a potential advertiser on a blog will require different information to a magazine editor, so your press kit should be tailored to your target audience. In general, though, a press kit should contain the following:

- Company information: a one-page background to your business.
- A short biography and what you have done before.

- A press release for your latest collection or product range. This must be as newsworthy as you can make it. Think about how your products connect with something relevant in the press at the moment, or consider what your products offer the wider market.
- An information sheet featuring details on your collection. Here, you want to include information about stockists, materials, and pricing.
- Contact details, so they can get in touch with you. Journalists and editors can be working to tight deadlines so be sure to include a phone number so they can contact you quickly if they need more information.
- Details of quality press you have received so far. Start with features in the national press, high-traffic blogs, and websites. This shows that the media is discussing your work. If you are just starting out (or don't have any press yet), use client testimonials to show what people think of your products.

- Cover letter. Your cover letter will bring together each element of your press kit in a pitch. Write a short introduction to your business, what your products are, and the benefits of them for your target customer. Then say where they can be found, what the press have been saying about you so far, and end with a call to action—what do you want the viewer of your press kit to do next? Contact you, make an order, or place an advert on your website?

PRESENTING YOUR PRESS KIT

Your press kit can be a digital PDF, which can be created using a design program. Using your best photos, consistent branding, and a large dose of your brand personality, you can put together a simple but effective kit. Turn it into a web-optimized PDF and you can not only email it out to prospective media, but also have it available on your website or blog for people to download.

If you want to create a physical press kit, you can get creative in how you present it. Think about your brand and products. You want your press kit to represent your brand, so if you're an eco-friendly business use materials such as kraft paper or cotton muslin bags; if you are a colorful children's brand, draw on this to inform your use of colors, materials, and typography. There are lots of ways to get creative with your press kit, but above all have fun with it and express your brand!

HOW TO GET PUBLISHED

7

Getting the right PR can be a game changer for your business, as it raises awareness of your brand and gets your name out there. PR for small businesses generally involves getting the word out about what you do. PR is about providing a story for the media—hopefully your story will inspire them to write about you, and then before you know it you'll be featured in all the best blogs, magazines, and newspapers, resulting in more sales.

The reality of PR is that it is a long-term strategy. You may get lots of sales following a feature in a national magazine, but this isn't always the case, especially with new brands. It takes time for people to trust small businesses. You have to work hard at getting them to switch from their usual supplier to your smaller, unknown brand. It's not impossible, but it takes time. Every feature or editorial will help you gain trust, but you need to show the benefits of shopping with you. Remember:

Raise awareness + build relationships = more sales

THINGS TO HAVE IN PLACE
BEFORE YOU SEEK PR

PRODUCTS PEOPLE WANT

Your products must be desirable to other people, not just you. Really consider whether your products are good enough to be seen beside big name brands and businesses because that's who you are competing with for editorial space.

A GREAT STORY

Saying "buy my stuff" is not an option any more. You need to share how you came to this point. Why do you do what you do? Your story is your differentiator from all the other businesses out there doing or selling the same thing as you.

HIGH-QUALITY PHOTOS

These must be high-resolution, clear and crisp, professional-looking shots that wouldn't be out of place alongside well-known brands. You may not be a photographer, but keeping things simple and in focus is a great start. You'll need a combination of lifestyle shots with your product in use (or in its natural scenery) and photos with a plain white background (for use as "cut outs") to enable magazines and bloggers to easily overlay your photos where they need them.

BUILDING YOUR PR STRATEGY

DETERMINE YOUR KEY MESSAGE

What are you trying to communicate? What is different about your business that you want to share with your audience? What makes you stand out from the crowd? Narrowing your message down to one or two main points will help keep you focused. What's your story?

In order to entice the media to write about you, they will expect a great story that their readers will resonate with. Think about why these people should write about you. What is it that makes your business different?

DEFINE YOUR TARGET AUDIENCE

This won't always be the same as the target market for your product. If you are selling children's clothes, you wouldn't aim your PR at children, but at the parents who will buy the clothes for their children. Think about who you want to reach and who will benefit most from what you have to offer.

CHOOSE THE BEST CHANNELS TO REACH YOUR AUDIENCE

You can choose from social media, magazines, radio, TV, YouTube, Instagram, Vine, and any other communication channel to get your message out there. Think about how your target audience consumes information. Where do you need to be seen?

BRAINSTORM TOPICS OF INTEREST

What topics can you tie your message to? Are there any public interest news stories happening at the moment that relate to your industry? What relevant topics can be associated with your products and business?

DETERMINE YOUR INFLUENCERS

Who influences your target audience? What magazines and blogs are they reading? Which bloggers or celebrities are they following and listening to? Once you determine who is influencing your target market, you can set out to build relationships with those people.

CULTIVATE YOUR MEDIA LIST

Once you know who your influencers are, you can start to cultivate your own personal media list. Your media list will contain contact details of all the blogs, newspapers, magazines, and radio stations that you wish to contact about your business.

SUBMIT THE RIGHT WAY, AND AT THE RIGHT TIME

Depending on who you are pitching to, you will have to follow their submission guidelines. Most blogs now have submission information on the site, while newspapers and magazines will also have the relevant information available. You need to follow their directions.

Magazines generally work two to six months ahead of the calendar, so they might approach you for their December holiday guides in June. Newspapers have a shorter lead time of around a month. Pitch well ahead of time, and be sure you've got the inventory you need at the right time—there is nothing worse than scrambling for products if the media needs something for a photoshoot. This also means planning any new product ranges well enough in advance so that you will be able to pitch them at the right time.

MONITOR RESPONSE AND EVALUATE

Keep track of who you submit to, their replies, and the outcome. Don't be discouraged if you don't hear back immediately—editors are busy people and won't always be able to reply straight away. Instead, focus on cultivating your list. You should always be adding to it and thinking of new places that may be interested in featuring your story.

It can take time to see results from your PR efforts and it is something that needs to be sustained over a period of time to get the best results.

EMPLOYING A PR COMPANY

The benefits of employing a PR firm to contact magazines and the press for you are that they know the industry and have lots of contacts already, whereas you're probably starting from scratch and already have many other things to focus on.

The fact is, trying to get your own publicity can be very time consuming. You need to respond to requests, send out photos and products, and keep track of who you have spoken to and when you are going to get your products back. Because of this, employing a PR firm is a great option (if you have the budget). The right company will have already cultivated relationships with the publications you want to be featured in, so it makes sense to pay to access them. This is especially true if being seen it the right magazines and getting press is important for your business.

Using a PR firm is best for entrepreneurs who have been in business for a while and those who are looking to reach a wider audience.

Print features can help you expand your customer base and raise awareness of your brand in your industry. If you want to be considered a key player in your niche—and to compete with big brands—then you need to be seen among them in the magazines your target market reads.

PR firms also have contacts with celebrity agents, so if you've always wanted to get your product in the hands of someone influential to your target customer, it might be easier through an agency.

DOWNSIDES TO HIRING A PR FIRM

PAYING FOR PR IS EXPENSIVE
You will likely have a team of people working to get editorial features for you. They will be using their network and relationships cultivated over years of being in business. All this is reflected in the price.

Possible solution: Working with freelance PR consultants can be cheaper than working with a company, but ensure they

have contacts in the industry and a great reputation. If their fees are not within your budget, you can still do your own PR—it might just take longer to get results.

YOU WILL STILL HAVE TO DO A LOT OF WORK
Even though your PR firm will do most of the work, such as contacting the media for you, you'll still need to do something yourself,

because their efforts should produce a lot of opportunities that you need to respond to. You might still need to send samples out to magazines, for example, follow up with email correspondence, attend PR events, and meet with magazine editors.

Possible solution: Try to do as much of the work in advance as possible. Put systems in place so you can respond quickly to PR requests. It is also a good idea to get your products ready beforehand and try to keep a flexible schedule.

PR IS RISKY

There are no guarantees that stories will run, or that the firm you choose to hire will be able to land your dream features. It also takes time to see results. While PR firms have a wide list of contacts, they still need to cultivate relationships and find the right opportunities for you, which takes time.

Possible solution: Decide on the minimum results you are looking for. If you are going to be spending thousands of dollars then you need to know what is the *least* you will be satisfied with. Any reputable PR firm should be able to tell you before you sign a contract if your goals are realistic or not. If the reality isn't something you are happy to go forward with, save your money.

HOW IT WORKS

Look for a PR firm with a proven track record in your field and with strong relationships with the press you want to be featured in. Look at their other clients to determine where they have been featured and what type of PR they received. While you want to choose a company that works with people in your industry, try to pick one without direct competitors. If you sell upcycled handbags made from coffee bags, for example, you don't want your PR team to be trying to get press for another company selling the same product. Each time they get an opportunity, they will have to choose between you and your rival.

You will likely have to pay a retainer each month, with the cost depending on the service they will be providing. The more they do for you, the more expensive it will be. As an estimate, you could expect to pay $800+ per month.

Retainer clients normally have to sign a minimum contract. Anything less than six months is not going to give you enough time to see if the PR is working, so it needs to be a long-term commitment. Magazines work months in advance, so you may not see the fruits of your PR investment for a while.

THE LAUNCH STRATEGY

⑦

Before you launch a new business, service, or product collection, you need to consider how you are going to let people know about it. No one wants to launch to silence and no interest—not only is it discouraging, but it won't make you any money! You want to create something buzzworthy that will help you achieve your launch goals.

SET GOALS FIRST

Having a clear strategy is crucial to a successful launch. Set your launch goals and be as clear as you can about what you want to achieve and how that fits in with your overall business vision. This is important as it will keep you focused and motivated through all your hard work.

CREATE A LAUNCH MAP

A launch map is a simple plan of what you have to do and by when. You can create it visually with sticky notes on your wall, or write everything down in a planner— whatever works best for you. The aim of the map is to make it easy to see what you need to work on. It also helps you space out the different activities you need to do and determine which order to do them in.

BE CREATIVE

The best launches are innovative. Try to come up with new ideas for your launch. People can become immune to companies always using the same tactics and strategies, so think of something different. If everyone in your industry launches using a specific email drip marketing campaign, try a different way to get the same results. How can you inspire your audience to take action and share your launch with their friends?

TAKE YOUR TIME

Don't rush out a new product, service, or collection. You need to put out the best work you can, so take your time to ensure the items work well with your brand and look cohesive. Set your launch date so you have enough time to do everything you need to.

PUT PEOPLE FIRST

Undoubtedly you will be excited about your launch, but put your target audience before the product. How does it benefit them? Don't just base your launch on how amazing your product or new service is—that won't inspire anyone—instead, focus on how your new product can improve their lives.

START HINTING

Build up anticipation for your launch by being sure to mention it whenever you can. Tell customers when you are working on something new. If you are interviewed for a blog or magazine, drop hints at new things that might be coming next. You can also do the same via social media. You don't have to be specific, though—the idea is to generate interest and set the scene for the future.

INVITE INDUSTRY INSIDERS

Whether you are launching online or hosting an event offline you need to ensure the media in your industry is all talking about your launch. If you are having a launch party, invite them. If you are launching online hold a virtual party, Twitter chat, or blog tour, and invite them to take part.

MAKE SURE THE PRESS HAVE THE RIGHT INFORMATION

You want to be in control of what is being reported, so make sure you supply full details to the media beforehand, and that influential press and bloggers have an up-to-date press release or press kit. Send them images they can use too, so once you have launched they are able to write about you without needing to ask for more information. Make it as easy as possible for them to write about you.

MAKE IT EXCLUSIVE

Invite select bloggers or your newsletter subscribers to view your new collection first. This will help create a buzz, especially if you encourage them to share their opinions with their networks. Supply them with great photographs and the opportunity for an exclusive interview.

DO SOMETHING UNEXPECTED

Consider ways that you can do something unexpected in your community or online. Make sure it fits in with the overall message you want to convey to your target audience.

THE ONE-PAGE MARKETING PLAN

The harder and more complicated your marketing strategy is, the less likely you are to implement it. You'll be more likely to stick to your marketing plan if you create something simple to work from that doesn't need a degree to understand. Marketing in its simplest sense is communicating the right message at the right time to the right people. That's it. Once you understand that, it becomes much easier to do effectively.

THE FOUNDATION OF YOUR MARKETING PLAN

RIGHT MESSAGE

Your marketing message is at the heart of all your marketing activity. It is what you will use to grab your target market's attention, so it needs to be on point, consistent, and simple enough so that the right people "get it." When crafting your message, you need to consider how your products will solve problems and why your target customer should buy from you instead of the other guy. That reason needs to be compelling enough for them to want to purchase, so look at the reasons why they buy and craft a message that touches on those reasons.

RIGHT TIME

It is important that your target audience sees your marketing message at the right time. Depending on your business this could be at the point of sale when they are ready to buy, or it could be at the research stage.

Take the wedding industry as an example. Most brides will look at wedding dresses for inspiration, even though they are not necessarily at the point of buying one right away. However, if they haven't seen your dress at the research stage—either through trying on dresses in a boutique or in a magazine—they are less likely to consider you at the point of sale.

Other businesses, such as a paper goods shop on Etsy, will need to convey their message right at the point their target customer is browsing. You can do this by making sure that your shop conveys your message through branding, photography, and product descriptions.

Consider the buying process that your customers normally takes. Do they buy on impulse, or does it take them numerous emails back and forth before they make a purchase? Be sure you are communicating your message at the relevant stage for it to be most effective.

RIGHT PEOPLE

It goes without saying that you can have the best product in the world, but if your target audience doesn't know about it (or want it for that matter), then you need to rethink your strategy.

Think clearly about who your target market is. Do the people you think want your product, really want it? Is the market full of products like yours? You will need to communicate how your product solves your target customer's problems. If the market is saturated with lots of competitors you may need to reassess your product offering to address this.

Once you have identified your true target market you will find it easier to reach them with your message. Where do they like to hang out? What blogs and magazines do they read? These are the places where you need your brand to be visible, either with features, advertising, or networking.

IDENTIFY THE MARKETING ACTIVITIES YOU WILL DO

Now that you have identified your message and who you will be targeting, it's time to identify the activities you can do to send your focused message out into the world.

LIMIT THE ACTIVITIES YOU CHOOSE

Marketing can easily become overwhelming for a lot of creatives, so go back to basics. Choose one marketing activity that you like doing and stick with that, developing how you use it so that you can increase its effectiveness. If up to now you have been using networking, blogging, PR, free consultations, and more to market yourself, choose one to work on, and master that before moving on to the next.

Social media is convenient and effective, but even within the social media category there is Twitter, Facebook, LinkedIn, Pinterest, and many other options that you can use to spread your message. Choose one or two to concentrate on—it doesn't matter which, just as long as you can interact with your target audience and you are comfortable using it.

LIMIT YOUR TIME ON THEM

Once you've chosen your activities, limit your time on them. Social media in particular can be a huge time waster if you aren't careful, so as part of a social media strategy, decide how long you are going to spend on it each day.

CREATE A STRATEGY AND STICK TO IT

The best way to keep your marketing simple is to create a strategy and stick to it. If you are networking, decide how many events you will attend each month, then keep to the plan. A strategy will ensure you don't panic and start holding sales when you should be adding value, or attending every local business event going, leaving you without time to work on other areas of your business.

WHY THE NEWSLETTER IS NOT DEAD

Every day we are bombarded with information and links. When you find a great blog or shop you can easily forget you ever saw it, as it gets pushed to the back of your mind only to be replaced with a slew of new information just a day or two later.

The problem is that the same thing is happening with your target customers. They see so many new shops and businesses that it's hard for you to stand out. Even when you do, they will quickly forget about you unless you are able to stay at the top of their minds.

Newsletters allow you to build a relationship with your customers and create a community around your products, while keeping it all within your control. While social network sites are great for creating a community, who knows what the future holds for Twitter and Facebook? In a year or two they may not be around, and the same goes for other social media tools. If these tools ended tomorrow, how would you be able to contact your customers?

In order for your customers to get on your email list, they sign up through an online opt-in form. This gives you permission to contact them with regular updates for as long as your reader is subscribed.

Newsletters can help you do that.

A newsletter is email correspondence that can potentially go out to thousands of people at the same time, as long as they are signed up to your email list. You can use an email provider such as MailChimp, set up a simple template, and just start writing. Put links on your website and share them with customers so they know you are using a newsletter as a way of staying in touch.

The focus is then on connecting with your target customer via their email inbox, so when they are ready to buy from you (or work with you), they remember your company above others. And it works.

CREATING A VALUABLE NEWSLETTER

DELIVER VALUE

The first step is to know how you are going to deliver value to your subscribers on a regular basis. You can offer exclusive content, resources, teach them a skill, or offer discount codes for your work. Whatever you send needs to put your subscribers' needs first. Make them want to open your emails.

BE AVAILABLE

One of the biggest benefits of sending out newsletters is that your readers can reply back to you. Allow them to do this by asking questions and trying to engage with them. You will get lots of great insights about what your real target market thinks, and it is an opportunity to offer more value and build on your relationship with them.

MAKE IT PERSONAL

Write to the reader directly, as though it is a personal email just to them. Share ideas of how they can use your products or how your services can benefit them.

SHARE SOME OF YOUR LIFE

Your newsletter subscribers want to feel like they know you, so share parts of your life with them. Did anything interesting happen that week or month? Think about any behind-the-scenes stories you can share. You don't have to get too personal, but true connections are built on trust and openness.

SHARE EXAMPLES OF CUSTOMIZED WORK

You can use your newsletter to share examples of work you have done for other people that may not make it to your website. Let them know you can be commissioned for customized work—they may not have realized this is something you do.

INTRODUCE NEW PRODUCTS AND SERVICES

Everyone loves to feel like they are the first to find out about new products. Give your subscribers sneak peeks at things you are working on, give them the option to pre-order, and send out discounts for loyal readers.

GIVE FREEBIES

You can send out a free gift that complements your products or services. It can be a PDF download, a checklist, or even tips and ideas that tie in with your products. Some ideas might include the first chapter of your book for free, desktop wallpaper featuring an inspirational quote, or printable gift tags.

BE PERSONABLE

Let your personality shine through. If your newsletter is full of sales speak, people won't want to read it. Be human and show the person behind the brand.

STARTING A BLOG

One of the best ways to promote your business and connect with potential customers, buyers, and boutiques is to write a blog. A blog is an online space where you can share your inspirations and ideas on a regular basis. Blogging is gaining momentum—especially amongst business owners—because it allows you to create content that aligns with your brand and entices people to read more about you and your work.

SETTING UP A BLOG

It couldn't be easier to set up a blog, as there are lots of free resources and blogging platforms available. If you are looking to test out blogging, I'd recommend blogger.com—a free platform that is easy to update. It also has lots of free templates and design choices.

If you want more control over the look of your blog (and are willing to pay a small amount per month for web hosting), I recommend Wordpress.org. It's slightly more complicated to set up, as you need to upload it through your hosting provider, but most have a one-click install option.

GETTING STARTED

CHOOSE A NAME FOR YOUR BLOG

If you already have a business name then use that to keep your brand consistent. If not, use your name and start building your personal brand as a business owner.

USE A CUSTOM DOMAIN

Link your blog to a custom domain and your website. You should already have the domain name for your business—if not, get it before someone else takes it. Using instructions from your blogging platform, you can use this domain to blog from as either joeblogs.com/blog or blog.joeblogs.com. Each provider is different, but they usually have a step-by-step guide on how to link a custom domain to your blog and a support team to help you with any questions you may have.

SELECT A TEMPLATE OR THEME

Blogger.com has free templates for you to use and tweak and you can find some beautiful Wordpress themes on woothemes.com. Remember that your blog will be another customer touchpoint for your brand, so keep the colors, fonts, and design style consistent with the rest of your visual branding.

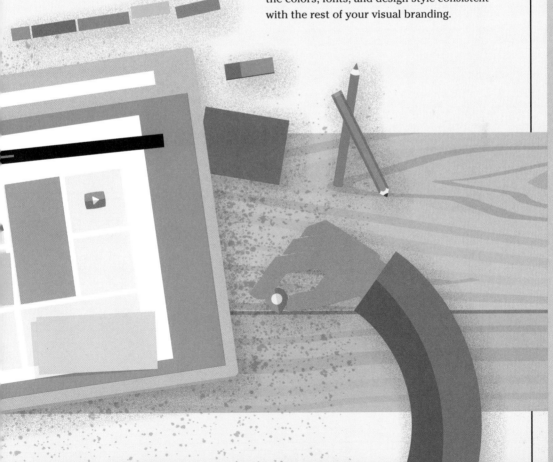

BLOGGING IS GOOD FOR BUSINESS

Writing regular content on your blog helps you rank higher in the search engines, which helps potential customers find you more easily. Be sure to use lots of keywords when you describe your work and what you do. Consider what topics your target market is searching for, then write blog posts around those themes. Use your blog as an opportunity to help customers make a decision about whether to buy from you or not. Showing your products styled in different ways, or how they fit in with current trends can be helpful to your target customer. It can also help you stand out from the competition.

Always reply to comments and engage with your readers. These will be potential customers, so they may have questions about your products and services that you'll need to answer. A well-managed blog can bring people one step closer to buying from you. Make them feel valued by taking an interest in what they write and always say "thank you."

WHAT TO WRITE ABOUT

Think about what questions and keywords your target market might be searching for. What questions do your customers ask you? How can you help them understand how you work and the benefits your product has? You can use blogging to answer all of these questions, and this will also help you get found more easily in the search engines.

You can also use your blog as a way to share what you are doing in your business. Share different parts of your process, your initial sketches, and photographs of your products.

You don't need to write a detailed step-by-step guide, or give away your secrets, but letting people see the work that goes into your products can help them understand their value.

You can also take your audience behind the scenes of your business, to show them the packaging and your studio, for example. Allow your readers and customers to find out more about you and to learn about your inspirations. Upload lots of photos and keep it visual.

HOW OFTEN SHOULD I BLOG?

Go for quality over quantity. As long as each post has a purpose and some value to your readers, it doesn't matter if you post once a week or every day—it's up to you. Do what you can manage without losing out on quality.

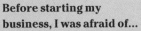

QUILL LONDON

WHO: Lucy Edmonds
WHAT: Stationery and paper goods shop
WEBSITE: www.quilllondon.com

Before starting my business, I was afraid of…

Failure! The fear that it wouldn't work out was the main thing that worried me, but I was also nervous about the massive life change I was undertaking. I left a "normal" 9–5 job, so I was giving up all the routines, systems, and everything I knew to take a leap into the unknown, which was pretty scary.

The one thing I wish I had known before starting my business…

Not to overthink things, and that no matter how much I plan, ultimately I have to let my business go its own way. It's a more organic process than I initially thought. I've seen that my business has taken its own path, leading me to new and unexpected places, which has been great.

My best tip for new creative business owners…

Plan, plan, plan! Having a strong business plan before you get going is essential, as it will help you to make as many mistakes as possible on paper, saving you any issues further down the line.

My favorite thing about running my own business…

The buzz I get every time someone orders something from my store can't be beaten. The fact that someone has chosen to spend their money in my store makes me feel so honored. I also love the amazing flexibility and variety in my daily routine. As a one-woman shop I do it all, from product photography to writing press releases and sending out orders. No day is ever the same.

CONTENT MARKETING

It might seem that "content marketing" is just the latest buzz phrase regarding business marketing, but unlike many new trends it actually works. In the simplest sense, content marketing means creating and distributing valuable and useful free content to your target customer, with the aim of converting them into buyers at a later date.

Content marketing works because you are focused on your target customer's needs and creating content that they will enjoy and find value in. This makes them keep coming back to your platform and engaging with you, which builds trust and can ultimately result in a sale.

You are not just selling or advertising in a broadcasting manner, instead you are creating content just as a publisher of a magazine or TV show would. Your content should be based on what you are selling. If you are an artist, think about how you can bring people into your world. What can your audience learn from you? How can you delight them? Maybe it could be with behind-the-scenes photos of you in your studio while you are painting, or process shots of how you build up color on a canvas.

The easiest way to provide content is through your blog or social media accounts—you might share weekly columns or daily photos of your products used in different ways. The content you create needs to be useful to your target market. People are busy. When they visit your website, blog, or social media accounts, they go there for a reason. Irrelevant content will make them tune out.

CREATING YOUR CONTENT STRATEGY

The first step in creating a content strategy that works is to focus on the customer. What do they want to see, read, or learn about? What can you write about or share with them that will help enhance their lives? What content can you create that only you have?

Nobody wants to engage with companies that are always shouting about their promotions. We don't get anything out of it. Content marketing is based on giving away free content that your target customer actually wants to see and be a part of. They are more likely to keep coming back to your website or blog when they know they will find something of interest to them there. It might seem counterintuitive to rarely promote your products, but if you are normally providing value, people are more likely to listen when you do have promotional content to share.

THE CONTENT TRIANGLE

Instead of trying to create content for all your social media sites and websites, focus on creating quality content that can be used in various ways on different platforms. I call this *the content triangle*.

At the base of the triangle is your main platform, which should be your website or blog. This is the place where you will send people from social media, networking, and advertising. Your base needs solid, top-quality content. It will last the longest here and you'll be driving traffic to these posts. The content you post here will be longer, more in depth, and you can try different things to keep it fresh.

Examples of great content for your blog or website might be a behind-the-scenes photo story of your process. You might also write some long articles answering questions your customers may have about your product, service, or industry.

The next level of the triangle consists of social media platforms, such as Twitter, Facebook, and YouTube. When you post here, your content gets indexed in search engines and is visible for longer than some of the purely visual social media out there.

Here you can post content that is both visual and text based, linking it back to your main platform and the more detailed content.

Using the example above, you could break the content down into smaller, bite-sized pieces that can be used on these platforms. So the photo story of your process can also be a short video story on YouTube or Vimeo. You can pull some images from your articles and post to Twitter and Facebook, along with a quote from your text or a short description. Use the opportunity to ask questions and engage with your followers.

The top of the triangle is reserved for visual social media like Instagram and Pinterest. These are fast moving, and while you can add text, it is not necessary unless you want to add a short description or some hashtags. Again, you can add photos here and link back to your main platform. Sticking with the previous example, you might take some images of your photo story and create a 10-second video for Instagram or Vine. You might also pull some quotes from your articles and make them into images to pin on Pinterest and share via Instagram.

VISUAL
INSTAGRAM
PINTEREST

VISUAL + TEXT
YOUTUBE, FACEBOOK,
TWITTER

YOUR BASE
YOUR WEBSITE OR BLOG

With each platform, link back to the website or blog at the base of your triangle.

SOCIAL MEDIA OUTREACH

With the social media landscape changing daily, rules and etiquette that were acceptable a few years ago just don't work in the same way anymore. If you have been on Twitter or Facebook lately, you will have noticed that people are interacting with each other less, and are instead shouting their latest offers and using marketing speak to try and entice customers. Broadcasting to your followers this way used to work, but now it puts many people off. You need to earn their attention by offering value instead. Shouting and making it all about you is not going to work—you need to give your followers a reason to listen to you.

WHAT IS "SOCIAL MEDIA OUTREACH"?

Instead of shouting, you should be using social media to reach out and engage one-on-one with potential customers. This makes them feel special and a part of something bigger, rather than just another customer number on a spreadsheet. While interacting in this way can take a bit more time, it is proving to be much more effective.

Most people think that all they need to do on social media is build their follower numbers, in the misguided sense that the more followers, the better. Instead of focusing on the followers they have, they will try to get more, even going so far as begging for "follows" and "likes" and paying to get new fans. Once they have these followers, they then schedule messages out to them in the hope that they will click through and buy something. It doesn't work.

The biggest benefit of social media is that you have the opportunity to engage individually with people all over the world. You don't need to have a huge budget—simply showing an interest in people can be a winning strategy. When someone follows you on social media, they are already interested in what you have to offer, so use their interest to start a conversation. Show that you are interested in finding out more about their needs.

Some examples of social media outreach are:

* Follow potential customers on different social media platforms. Look at people following your competition and add some of them each day. Some of these will follow back if it looks like you have something of value to offer.

- Ask questions (generally to your followers, but also directly to individual fans). Even asking how their day is going is a great conversation starter.
- Show appreciation on their social posts. Favorite their Tweets (especially if they mention your company), like their photos on Instagram, and Retweet things that your followers might be interested in.
- Use their Tweets to start a conversation. Comment on something they have said.
- Visit their blog, leave a comment that adds to the conversation, and share their blog with your followers.

- If they ask a question and you know the answer, answer it. It's another opportunity to stand out by offering value.
- Use the same tactics for social media influencers, bloggers, tastemakers, and editors in your industry. Be sure you are adding value and being helpful, and you will build relationships without having to be false.
- By acting like a person, rather than a company, you will open yourself up to building relationships.

HOW MANY SOCIAL MEDIA SITES SHOULD I BE ON?

It can be hard to keep up a presence on every social media channel, but at the very least you should be sure to secure your company name on each one. Then consider where your target audience is consuming content. You need to be where they are, but also balance that with using the social media sites that feel most natural to you. Ideally, you will have a website or blog as your main platform, with at least one social media site from each layer of the content strategy triangle.

YOU

GROW
YOUR
BUSINESS

SCALING YOUR BUSINESS

⑧

After you have been in business a while you will start to consider where you want go next. What do you want to achieve? What are the next goals you want to achieve? For many business owners, growth is the next step, which means more customers, more visibility in their industry, and more profit.

Most creative entrepreneurs work primarily alone and struggle when it comes to growth. Usually it is just you running the business and every aspect that entails. You may find yourself filling many roles from designing new products, taking photographs, making the products, and then promoting them. Freelancers often offer services that rely on them, personally, making it difficult to grow the business beyond a certain point. Makers also have this problem as they can only make

so many things in the time available. After a while, you may reach a point when you have too much work or too many orders to fill.

At first, you may end up turning orders away, closing your shop to catch up, or starting a waiting list for keen customers. However, these are all short-term solutions. If you want your business to grow in the long term, you need to ensure you have systems in place that will allow you to scale.

Scaling a business refers to being able to replicate the business model to make more money. Even if you think you will always be happy with you business earning a certain salary for you, think about the future.

WHAT IS YOUR LONG-TERM PLAN?

Your goal might be to always make every item by

hand. That is fine, but you can increase your income in other ways, such as getting help with the admin side of the business, freeing up more time for you to make your products. Or you can offer different products that don't rely on you to increase your income. You can also sell patterns, kits, and digital ebooks related to your subject of expertise, or host workshops or making evenings. Be creative. Diversifying your income stream can give you the flexibility to grow your business and increase your profits.

DELEGATE

Creative entrepreneurs generally like to be in control of their lives and careers. This can make it hard to let go and trust someone else to do things for you. For so long, you have only had to rely on yourself to get things done, meaning it can be difficult to let go enough to teach someone else how to do those tasks.

Delegating frees you up to concentrate on the parts of the business you enjoy the most and that only you can do. In order to be more efficient with your time you need to ensure that your time is being spent wisely. Only do the jobs that no one else can do for you.

You may actually be surprised at how little this is. Packaging, accounts, paperwork, even hiring someone to clean your house can be contracted out and free up time that you can spend on tasks that need your specific talent or skill.

Of course, contracting these things out costs money, so they may not be suitable for everyone. However, if you are working every waking hour, turning down work because of a lack of time, and still not making enough to pay someone else to do some of the work, your business will never be able to grow.

SYSTEMS

Systems can also help you to scale up your business. Everything you do more than once for your business can be developed into a system. This means it can be followed not just by you, but by anyone who has the details. Write down step-by-step processes for every aspect of your business. Not only will this make it easier for you to delegate the job to someone else, but it will also save you time when you do it, as you won't have to decide what to do next.

RECONSIDER YOUR PRODUCT LINE

Is there a way you can streamline your processes? Maybe you can make more products at a time, or balance out your items with less time-consuming ones. For example, if you paint original artwork, maybe you could also sell prints, greeting cards, and postcards featuring the same artwork.

INCREASE PRICES

If your work is in demand and you can't take on any more, put your prices up—this is the only way you will make a comfortable living doing what you love. You may sell less, but you will charge more, so you'll still have the potential to grow in the future. You will also have the means to pay someone else to help you out when necessary.

Hopefully, you are now thinking about how you can grow your business when the time is right. It may seem a long way off, but considering your options now can save you disappointment in the future.

KEEPING YOUR VISION AS YOUR BUSINESS EVOLVES

So things are going great for you, your business is doing well, you are making sales, and you are wondering what is next. You look online and see your competitors have a new product or service and you think "I can sell that!"

This is "shiny object syndrome."

As your business grows and develops it is only natural to want to try new things, but you need to be aware of *why* you want to try

them. Is it because you really feel this is the best next move for you? Or are you being swayed by what others are doing? Not all opportunities will be right for you, your business, and your brand.

HOW TO KEEP YOUR VISION

The best way to keep your vision as your business evolves is to keep returning back to your core values and always developing new products, services, and business strategies based on those. Your core is what makes you different and is why your customers do business with you, so don't alienate them by deviating from your core values just because someone else is doing something different.

CLARIFY YOUR LONG-TERM VISION AND SHORT-TERM VISION FOR YOUR COMPANY

The long-term vision is where you want to be in ten years' time. Your short-term vision is where you want to be next year and the one you will work toward on a daily basis. You could also try a mid-term (five-year) vision.

Translate your short-term vision into smaller goals and build daily, weekly, and monthly action plans from that.

THINK SMALL (FOR NOW)

Thinking big is all the rage, but it can also stop people from moving forward. If you feel as if you are diverting away from your initial vision, go back to thinking small for a moment. What is the next, best step for your company?

REDEFINE YOUR CORE

Your core is the heart of the company and will shape how you decide to grow and the decisions you make along the way. You might make the choice to refocus your product range to what excites you the most and what you are most passionate about.

GOING GLOBAL VS. STAYING LOCAL

Growing a creative business can mean different things to different people. For you, it might mean increasing production, getting more sales, outsourcing tasks, or revisiting your pricing structure so you can make more profit. It could also mean growing your audience on your social media networks or blog.

When it comes to business growth, there is no single definition that is right for everyone, and what works for expanding one company may not necessarily be the best way to grow another business. It can be easy to get swayed by what other people are doing in your field—if you have successful competitors, you might see their success as the only way to do things. But most often, it is not.

DEFINE GROWTH ON YOUR TERMS

The first part of deciding the type of growth you would like for your business, is defining what growth looks like for you. Is it based on a turnover level? A level of recognition in the industry or within your target market? Maybe you think of growth in terms of graduating from selling direct to consumers to wholesaling your products to large retailers, such as department stores? You might want to get to a level where you can outsource all your manufacturing so you can make more products at a better profit margin. Alternatively, growth could be something you think of in terms of how you will grow as a business owner—personal growth is just as important to consider as professional growth.

Whatever growth looks like for you, you need a vision, or a deeper purpose for what you do. Look back over your vision and goals. What are you aiming for? How will you know when you reach it?

Growing your business with intention is about carefully considering your business—the vision, the scalability, the business model—and asking how you can best create a long term, sustainable business that brings you joy and contentment. You may want to keep your business small and only work directly with clients yourself, or you might want to become a household name. There is no right or wrong. It's up to you to decide what it is you want from your business and set out to achieve it. Be yourself and grow your business your way.

The growth you aim for should be based on your vision for your company and not what other people want and expect you to do. If you don't want to wholesale your products, don't do it. If the idea of growing your freelance business into a full-blown agency sounds like your worst nightmare, don't do it. As long as you are basing your decision on what you truly want, rather than deciding based on fear of the unknown or not wanting to get out of your comfort zone, then stick to your dreams.

LOCAL

DO YOU HAVE TO GROW?

I think you have to grow. Over time, your skills get better, your relationships deepen, and your understanding of your customers develops and grows. Your offerings will change and you will grow as a person. It's naive to think you won't develop and evolve on your journey as a business owner. You may be happy where you are right now, but do you really want things to be exactly the same in 20 years' time?However, growing your business doesn't have to mean earning more money, taking on employees, and building a huge empire. It can also mean taking considered steps to develop your business and your skills over time, in a way that feels right for you.

HOW TO DEVELOP LONG-TERM GOALS

When we think about setting business goals we often look to the immediate future of what we want now or next. When you are starting out, your goals are often simply to open your shop, get your first client, and other steps that will get you started on your business journey. Even if you have an idea of what you want your business to look like in the future, it often doesn't translate into your long-term, goal-setting strategy.

USE YOUR VISION

Your vision is your anchor. It gives you a focus and a means of staying on the right track to achieve your goals. Consider what you want to achieve as part of the bigger picture for your company, and develop goals that will take you there.

THINK AHEAD

When you set long-term goals you need to think about what your life might be like further on in your journey. It can be difficult to imagine, especially as life never goes entirely to plan, but don't just think about right now—what life changes or milestones do you hope to achieve? Do you want to have children, go traveling, and/or have homes in every continent? How you want your life to look like in five, ten, or 30 years' time will impact on your long-term business goals.

THINK ABOUT LEGACY

How do you want to be remembered? Do you want people to have physical things to remember you by, such as the products and art you have designed and created? Or is an intangible, non-visible legacy enough?

We're all leaving a legacy behind, just by existing in the world. We'll be remembered by the people dearest to us, but we can also be intentional about the legacy we leave behind. What type of legacy do you want to leave? Maybe you want to inspire others to make an impact in the world? You can do this through the products and services you offer and through leading by example and making an impact with your own work.

Of course, your legacy isn't just about the work you leave behind, it's also about the person you were, the way you made people feel, and the things you created in your spare time. So if you are working as an employee, but you paint every weekend, those paintings will be a part of your legacy. You don't have to sell your art for it to mean something.

WHAT WILL MAKE YOU HAPPY?

Happiness means different things to different people. It could be having lots of money, or spending quality time with your loved ones, or it could be sitting in a tent on a mountaintop. It doesn't matter what makes you happy (legal things only though, please!), as long as you find it.

So how can you find what makes you happy? By doing things. By taking risks and saying "yes" to things you would normally say "no" to; by taking a chance on something new and exploring new territories; by making new friends and reaching out to different people; by getting out of your comfort zone and accepting opportunities and projects that you may normally shy away from. Use this to guide your vision and long-term goals, and create plans to help you achieve the things most important to you.

COLLABORATING WITH OTHER CREATIVES

There is something magical that happens when creative entrepreneurs collaborate. Having another person with a different skill set to bounce ideas off can take creativity to a new level. You might feel that you still have so much to learn as a business owner before anyone would want to collaborate with you, but collaborations can work no matter where you are in your business journey—you just need to look for the opportunities and be willing to go after them.

THE BENEFITS OF COLLABORATING

Aside from wonderful new ideas that you may never have come up with alone, collaborating can help strengthen your relationships with other creatives, improve your skills, and increase your revenue. As a team you can work on bigger projects by pooling resources, time, and money, which means even though you will have to split the profit, you can often reach much higher revenue goals than you could alone.

IDEAS FOR COLLABORATING

SKILLS MATCH

One of the most popular ways for creatives to collaborate is by bringing different skills together to make an unstoppable team. Maybe you are a designer and they are a web developer—together you can work on projects offering a full web design and development service. Perhaps you are a photographer and you bring your skills to a project with a stylist and stationery designer to produce photoshoots for editorials in wedding magazines or stylish events. The possibilities are endless.

PRODUCT MATCH

Is there a way you can match your products with someone else's to create a set or gift package? If you sell woven bowls for example, you could team up with an organic soap company to offer gift sets or wedding favors. Consider which products would work well with yours and research other creatives you can approach with a proposal. The best product matches are when two (or more) items come together to create an even more valuable purchase for the buyer.

BUILD A TEAM

Collaborations don't have to be limited to a couple of people. Creatives have had lots of success coming together and creating conferences, craft fairs, and collectives.

A group can open many more opportunities and will have bigger networks to help bring everything together.

THE KEY TO SUCCESSFUL COLLABORATIONS

The key to successful collaborations is finding the right personalities to collaborate with—it doesn't work well with just anyone. When you approach people, make sure they are a good fit by meeting for coffee and discussing your ideas. You could also do a few informal projects first, which will let you see how you like working together before you jump into something big.

EXPANDING WITH INTENT

8

When you approach your business with intent, and consider the wider purpose behind what you do, it provides an anchor, or a guide stick, with which to measure all your decisions against. It also helps you stay on track because you know what you are ultimately aiming for and why.

DESIGN THE BUSINESS YOU WANT

Grow your business with intent by defining what you want your business to look like. Design the business that you have in mind and that aligns with your vision, rather than how you think a business in your industry needs to look. One of the benefits of creating your own business is that you get to decide how to do things. If every other business in your industry promotes their business in a certain way, you can choose to do things differently. Go against the grain and your company will stand out from the crowd.

STAY IN TUNE WITH YOUR PURPOSE

The second step is to revisit the purpose of your business—the foundation on which your company was founded. Be clear about what you stand for and create a business manifesto. It doesn't have to be made public, but it can help you redefine what it is your business intends to do, your principles, and your values.

DON'T RUSH IT

Once you have decided that you want to expand your business, it can be tempting to rush things to reach your goals as soon as possible. If you grow too fast, you could find it hard to keep up with orders, or you may find that your systems are not able to work at that level. Pace yourself. Allow yourself time to expand a bit at a time. Set milestones so you can assess how things are going at each major growth stage.

INVESTING IN EXPANSION

Growing your business can be costly. You will need to reinvest finances back into the business to allow for growth. Depending on your goals, your expansion may require employees or premises.

That money has to come from somewhere. Save as much as you can along the way and limit your reliance on business loans. While they can sometimes be unavoidable, business loans or outside investment can add extra pressure to your emerging company. Be sure to get legal advice before taking on any loans or partnering with investors.

REDDSKIN LONDON

WHO: **Karen Arthur**
WHAT: **Fashion and accessories designer**
WEBSITE: **www.reddskin.co.uk**

Before starting my business, I was afraid of...

So many things, but mostly falling flat on my face! Fear of not being good enough. Fear that the only people who would buy my designs would be related to me. That lack of confidence has stopped me from moving forward with my business on many occasions—I realize that I'm a "slow burner," but also that I weigh things up before jumping in. I used to see this as a fault, but I now know that it works for me.

The one thing I wish I had known before starting my business...

That I can't do everything by myself. Do the things you're great at and pay people to do the things you aren't good at or hate. I have wasted so much time procrastinating over aspects of my business that I'm not very good at when I should have just offloaded the work and concentrated on doing what I love!

Also that just because you get one thing "wrong" doesn't mean that you've failed—every stumbling block is also a learning experience that helps you become better.

My best tip for new creative business owners...

If you can't do it, outsource it. So much of my creative time has been wasted on, for example, tax returns and accounts (ugh), when I am fully aware it's my least favorite thing and I have little skill in this area. It's money well spent when you can pay people to do the stuff you hate.

My favorite thing about running my own business...

I love sewing, designing, and teaching. To be on my way to making a living from all three and make decisions about how I spend my time is probably the best part. I'm taking control of my own life... and it feels empowering.

WHEN TO GET AN OFFICE OR STUDIO SPACE

8

When you started out, you thought that working from home would be the greatest. You could work in your pajamas, cook a nice hot lunch everyday, and make as many cups of coffee as you need throughout the day, no spare cash required. As time has gone on though, you realize that working from home is starting to get out of hand. Your dining table is no longer cutting it and your work piles are taking over the house. So when is the right time to move into an office space?

There will never be the perfect time to move. There will always be a reason (usually financial), to keep you working from home for as long as possible. It's up to you to decide when to take the leap and if you can afford it.

HOW TO KNOW IF YOU'RE READY

REGULAR SALES/CUSTOMERS
If you are getting regular sales and clients, to the point that your income is growing every month, you might be ready to move out of your home. Think about the benefits. If the money you spend on business premises means you can get more work done—and therefore increase your earnings—then it could be an option for you.

MONEY IN THE BANK

If you have funds in the bank to invest in an office or studio space then the biggest barrier to breaking away from being a homeworker is negated. Most entrepreneurs stay working from home because they can't afford another option. If you have the money and you think it would be a wise way to spend it (the benefits outweigh the cost), then go for it.

YOUR HOUSE IS NO LONGER CUTTING IT

Some work needs more space than others. A freelance copywriter will need less space than a craft blogger who might need space to store craft materials, a place for photoshoots, and somewhere to host small workshops, for example. If working from home is stopping you from expanding your services, or your materials are taking over the house, a studio space outside the home could be just what you need.

YOU NEED SPACE FOR YOUR TEAM OR CLIENTS

If you are expanding your team, you may not have the space or the inclination to have them all working from your home. It can get cramped pretty quickly, which can have a negative effect on working relationships. Alternatively, you might need somewhere for client meetings when the coffee shop just isn't appropriate anymore.

OPTIONS TO CONSIDER

Depending on your budget and needs, you might consider shared studio space or shared office space. You could also rent your own studio if you need more room and/or have a big team and lots of materials or equipment.

If you sell products, you could consider a retail shop with an office space, so you can have everything under one roof.

CO-WORKING SPACES

If you aren't quite ready to move into your own studio space with a contract and regular rent payments, you could try a co-working space. Lots of co-working studios are appearing now, as many creative entrepreneurs are location independent and can work wherever there is Wi-Fi.

The main benefit of co-working studios is that they often have different membership levels depending on your usage needs, which makes it affordable for most entrepreneurs. You will also regain a social aspect to your work by meeting other creatives that work there. Co-working spaces also often host classes so you can learn new skills.

BUILDING YOUR TEAM

The look of your team will depend on the type of business you run and the needs that you have. A freelance designer might have too much work and offer it to another designer under contract, for example, while a fashion designer might contract out the production of their products to local seamstresses or a factory when the orders become too much to handle alone. You might decide to put off hiring your first employees if you don't have the money to pay them yet, but even so, you don't have to jump straight into becoming an employer to expand your team.

There is a misconception that you should put off growing your team until you have been in business a while or until you have no option but to expand. This isn't always the best thing for a business, though—you can't grow a business alone in a vacuum. You need to build a team to help you. At the very least you need to bring on board people with the professional skills that you don't have. This could be accountancy skills or a lawyer. Even if these are not part of your permanent team, working in your office, they are still helping you reach your business goals.

WHAT SKILLS DO YOU LACK?

The best way to start building your team is to look out for the skills that are missing. Be honest about what you can do best and think about what roles you need to add to the business. If you struggle with marketing your business, then you could add a marketing consultant or social media maven to your team. You don't need to employ them full time, or at all at this point—most freelancers will invoice you per project or you can work with them on a retainer basis. It means you don't need to start out with lots of extra funds to grow your team.

LOOK FOR PEOPLE WHO BELIEVE IN YOUR VISION

For your team to work well, everyone needs to be on the same page when it comes to your company vision and goals. When you are looking for the right people to fill the skills gap, make sure they understand what you are trying to achieve with the business. It will only cause problems later if you bring in people who have a different idea about the best way to grow your business. If not discussed and clarified at the start of the relationship, you could get a surprise later when one of your team members makes a decision you don't agree with!

THE GREEN GABLES

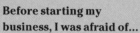

WHO: Gabrielle Treanor
WHAT: Stationery designer
WEBSITE: www.thegreengables.co.uk

Before starting my business, I was afraid of...

Failure! I was scared I wouldn't be able to make a success of working for myself and I'd have to go back to my old life, which didn't fulfill me, light me up, or let me live the way I truly wanted to.

The one thing I wish I had known before starting my business...

It takes longer than you think to make money. I thought I had planned and researched, but it took a lot longer than I anticipated to really begin to make money. That doesn't mean that you need to have years of savings before you think of quitting a steady income, just have contingency plans in case you don't earn as much as quickly as you'd hoped.

My best tip for new creative business owners...

Get help with the stuff you're no good at or have no interest in. Just because you haven't a clue about accounting or hate the thought of marketing doesn't mean you can ignore them. Concentrate on what you do best—or what you're interested in learning about—and then find people to help you with the other vital stuff.

My favorite thing about running my own business...

I do things exactly as I choose to and I don't have to compromise on things that are important to me. If I want to stick to my ethics—even if it means making life more complicated or difficult—it's my decision to do so. I listen to other people's advice, opinions, and feedback, but when it comes down to it, I make the decisions about how my business is run and therefore how I live my life.

EMPLOYEES, VIRTUAL ASSISTANTS, INTERNS, AND FREELANCERS

Building your team doesn't necessarily have to start with your first "official" employee. There is a number of different ways that you can utilize the skills of others in your business.

EMPLOYEES

Taking on your first employee can be daunting, which is why many small business owners tend to try virtual assistants, interns, or freelance contractors first. However, there will come a time when you need an employee to do the work, either because you need someone full time or because a salaried role would be more cost effective.

Don't hire an employee until you have regular work for them, though. This doesn't just mean when you have "a bit of work," but when you have so much that you are having to turn down work on a frequent basis.

You will also need to check out your legal requirements before taking on your first employee. You will likely need to supply a contract, salary, employee benefits, disciplines and grievance procedures, and have a means to do payroll with the correct tax deductions.

Your employees don't have to work in your office unless you need them to—many people are available to work from home or online. Even if they are predominantly working from home, you may still prefer your employees to be local, so you can meet up occasionally.

VIRTUAL ASSISTANTS

Employing the services of a virtual assistant can be a flexible way to get some help in your business. You can set the number of hours per week and the tasks, with the benefit of only paying them for the amount of time they work on your projects.

A virtual assistant can perform a variety of administrative support, such as answering emails, research, customer support, and even organizing and planning your schedule for you. As the work is done online, your virtual assistant can be based anywhere in the world, which means you aren't limited by the talent in your local area.

For the virtual assistant relationship to work well, you need to set clear instructions and tasks per week so they can get on with the job. This makes it ideal for task-related work that can be measured and assessed. You can find virtual assistants through recommendations or dedicated sites such as oDesk.

INTERNS

In certain industries, such as fashion, design, and blogging, internships seem to be the prevalent way to expand your team. Internships can be paid or unpaid, and are usually temporary, making them best suited to people looking to get experience in a certain field.

Before you decide on offering an internship it is important that you look at the legalities in your country or state. Just because other people are offering them, doesn't make it legal. Unpaid internships normally need to adhere to very clear rules—expenses have to be paid and there must be learning involved through work shadowing. Your intern shouldn't be doing the role of an employee.

You can arrange internships through colleges or by advertising on your website. Many colleges allow students to collect credits for their course if the work is relevant to their studies.

FREELANCERS

Collaborating and working with freelancers is another popular way to expand a team. Designers often team up with other freelancers to offer an holistic range of services, such as web design, development, marketing, and copywriting.

You can also employ the services of a freelance marketing consultant or strategist to help you with your business, or a photographer to create beautiful photos

of your products without you having to officially take them on as an employee.

Freelancers set their own rates, but many are flexible and open to collaboration on projects. You can find freelancers to work with through social media and portfolio sites such as Behance.

HOW TO FIND THE RIGHT EMPLOYEES AND HIRE THEM

When you are ready to employ your first employee you can go about it in a number of ways. You can advertise the job specification on your website, then share the link, asking if anyone knows someone with the right skills who would be interested. You could also advertise the job with a recruitment agency, so they can check all the applicants and send the best ones over to you to interview.

WHERE TO FIND THEM

ASK FOR RECOMMENDATIONS

One of the easiest ways to hire someone is to ask for recommendations. You can do this in real life or via social media. You can share the job description and application link and ask if they know anyone that could be a good fit. If you are looking for someone local that can make it to your office each day, asking around friends and family in your area could be beneficial.

HIRE A PAST CLIENT OR CUSTOMER

If you've been in business a while, you'll have customers and clients who might be a good fit. If you have already worked together, they will already be familiar with how you work and your company. This can especially work if your clients are freelancers with different skills to yours. They may be looking for extra work, or a permanent opportunity.

POST YOUR POSITION ON A RECRUITMENT WEBSITE

A third option is to post your position on a recruitment website or jobs board for your industry. This can expose your listing to many interested candidates. You may need to pay to list your position and not all sites will sift through candidates for you, so be sure to check what service you're getting for the listing price. Be clear about the qualifications and skills needed so you only get relevant candidates applying.

RECRUITMENT ESSENTIALS

Regardless of how you go about finding an employee, the position you are offering will need the following:

- a job specification
- job role and duties
- salary
- hours of work
- experience required

THE APPLICATION PROCESS

Using an application form or other process will help you to filter out the right candidates for your position. To ensure you get the best people, you need to ask more questions than just those relating to experience. As you are building a small, effective team, you need to make sure the people you hire will fit in to your company, have the same work ethic, and fill the skills gap that you have.

QUESTIONS TO ASK

In addition to questions about experience and relevant qualities, it is useful to try and distinguish similar candidates by asking them what ideas they have for your company or their skills outside of the job specification. Some questions you might ask are:

- Why do they want to work with you?
- What ideas do they have about a new product or service for your brand?
- What are their strengths?
- What are their weaknesses?

CREATING A COMPANY CULTURE

You might think that creating a company culture is the least of your worries when you are trying to start and grow your business, but leaving it to chance can be damaging to your success in the long term. Even if you think it might be a while before you add new members to your team, developing a clear company culture will make it easier when the time comes.

A thriving company culture creates a cohesive team all working towards the same goal. Productivity is higher when people feel valued and a part of a greater vision.

LOOK TO THE FUTURE

The reason that so much business strategy starts with your ultimate vision for your company is because it is important that everything you do is focused on your end goal. What will your company look like in ten years? How do you work together as a team? What things are important to you and your employees? How do you get them excited about their work and your vision? Once you have some answers you can start paving the way to creating the culture you envision.

CULTURE AND BRANDING

Your company's culture will reflect your brand in the same way that your brand identity or website does. Your brand values, personality, and goals will be shared with your culture. How can you express it within the workplace? How can you ensure your employees understand and feel passionate about how you work and what you believe?

SHARE YOUR VISION WITH YOUR EMPLOYEES

For your employees to feel like they are part of the bigger picture, they need to know what it is you are striving for. This goes beyond revenue goals and back to purpose. Why does your company exist? What impact are you trying to make on the world and how can you translate this to your employees? Maybe you infuse sustainability in everything you do, from your products, to the green energy you use, to your recycling program? Make it clear what your company is about, and let your employees be a part of it. Allow them to suggest ideas.

IT'S WHAT YOU DO, NOT WHAT YOU SAY

As much as you can talk about values, it's what you do and how you treat people that really creates the culture in your workplace. If you say you value family, but make it hard for your employees to spend time with their families around the holiday season, your culture will suffer. Implement your company's values into every part of your business, right from the start. When you take on your first employee, you will already know what benefits to offer that reflect the culture and values you want your company to embody.

BONUS

HOW TO ASSIGN AND DELEGATE

When you start adding people to your team you will need to learn how to delegate. Whether you like it or not, you'll be the boss. In order to get the most out of your employees you will have to learn how to be an effective leader. If you have been working for yourself for a while, it can be hard to then add team members into the mix that you have to give work to, but in order for your business to grow you need to learn how to make it work.

LEARN TO LET GO

You need to forgo the idea that you are the only person in the entire world that can do what you do. There is always something you can delegate and if you don't have faith in your employees, they will soon leave. It's up to you to relinquish some of the control you have and allow them to make their mark on their tasks.

DECIDE WHAT CAN BE DELEGATED

Before you start to delegate you need to decide what it is that you still want to do. What are you best at? How do your employees' skills fit into the mix? Ideally, you want to recruit people whose skills complement yours so that it is easier to assign tasks to them that they can do better than you. When deciding between tasks that can and can't be delegated, think about what you want to be known for. If you want to be known as the jewelry designer for your brand, then retain the majority of design tasks and pass on anything else to your employees.

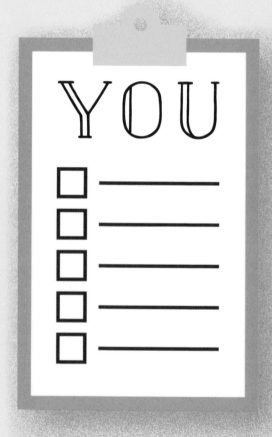

MAKE IT EASY FOR THEM TO DO THE JOB

Part of delegating is teaching someone to do the tasks how you want them. Make it easy for them by putting together an employee handbook or manager book full of processes, tasks, and systems. This will enable you to pass the baton to new employees a lot more smoothly. It gives them something to refer back to, make notes in, and ask questions about, rather than waiting for them to find their way on their own. You will also save time in the long run because you won't have to keep going over the system, again and again. If you can make it easier for your team to get the job done, your business will thrive.

ASSIGN THE RIGHT TASKS TO THE RIGHT PEOPLE

Ensure you get to know your employees and their skill sets before delegating any new tasks to them. One of the main reasons delegation fails is because the wrong person was chosen for the job. If you have any doubt about a person's ability to do the job, choose someone else. Listen and observe to see who can do what—sometimes people can surprise you. If you want to know if someone can do a job to your standards, ask them. Give them a trial run or test and see how they handle it. The objective here is to have faith in others and to give them time to learn the ropes.

SET BOUNDARIES

When assigning jobs to team members, you need to make sure there are clear outcomes and boundaries for each task. If there are unacceptable ways of doing something, then make it known to avoid confusion. In the same vein, if there's a certain amount of flexibility in how they achieve a goal, let them know. As long as the final outcome is achieved, offering flexibility can encourage employees to be more creative.

WHAT TYPE OF LEADER DO YOU WANT TO BE?

(8)

When you decide to expand your team beyond yourself, you need to consider what type of leader you want to be. You might be scoffing right now, saying, "Leader! I'm not a leader, I just want to run my business!" But in order to bring your team together and get the most from it, you need to lead.

While it sounds nice to think of your company as being full of your friends, the reality is that it is your business and livelihood. You are responsible for paying other people and ensuring the best products, services, and customer service to your customers. To get your employees or team to do the best work, you need to lead them in the direction you want them to go.

FOCUS ON HELPING PEOPLE GROW

Being an effective leader isn't about how well you perform—it's about how well your team are able to perform under your guidance. Businesswoman, author, and blogger, Penelope Trunk, says the role of any good leader is to help turn people into stars. "Management is essentially an act of constant giving and constant patience. It entails giving people a little attention all of the time, instead of giving them lots of attention only when they mess up. In fact, if you're managing people effectively they don't mess up, because you play to their strengths and teach them how to move around their weaknesses."

Hands-off management isn't respectful— it's negligent. People want mentoring and guidance from their manager. If you give that in a way that helps them grow, while also treating them with respect, they'll love having you around. And when your direct reports love having you around, they do their best work for you out of loyalty.

LEAVE THEM TO IT

The main benefit to having employees that you can delegate tasks to is that you don't have to do the tasks yourself. Being an effective leader means being able to leave them to get the job done without constantly looking over their shoulder. Once you have trained any new staff, your employee handbook—with all your processes and systems—should have enough information so they can get on with the job without having to ask you every little thing.

LET THEM USE THEIR SKILLS

The people you employ are likely to be multi-passionate and multi-talented, just like most creatives. If they have extra skills that you could use in some way, let them use them. Giving your employees the chance to shine will help them feel secure and valued as a team member, even if the skills they are using are not essential to their current role. Encouraging them to develop their skills and be creative can help them problem solve for your business in new and exciting ways that you might never have thought of otherwise.

"If your ACTIONS inspire others to DREAM more, LEARN more, DO more and BECOME more, you are a LEADER."

JOHN QUINCY ADAMS

LIFE
AS AN
ENTREPRENEUR

MANAGING EXPECTATIONS: ENTREPRENEUR MYTHS

There are many myths surrounding what entrepreneurs do, how they make money, how they work, and who they work with. The general public has a certain view, as do the many "wantrepreneurs"—those people who want to become an entrepreneur because it sounds good or they see others doing it and want to do the same thing.

The reality is, running a business is hard. You will work long hours (especially at the start, when you are establishing yourself) and you will need to do almost everything yourself unless you can trade a service or get a friend or family member to help you out. You are not going to be lounging in your pajamas all day, or get featured in Oprah Magazine in your first week—here are some other myths that need to be exploded:

YOU WILL MAKE LOTS OF MONEY

Sorry to shatter the dream, but not every entrepreneur is going to become the next Mark Zuckerberg, and it will take time for you to make money. Starting out, your income will ebb and flow, and one of the biggest challenges entrepreneurs face is that their income is not guaranteed. Not knowing where the next rent payment is coming from, or if you will have any sales in the next month can be stressful. However, it can also motivate you to work harder and succeed.

YOU HAVE LOTS OF SPARE TIME

Running your own business means you set your own schedule, yes, but it also means you can end up working too much because you know that when you're not working, you're not earning money. Having access to social media and email via your phone can mean

it's a struggle to switch off at night or when the weekend comes—the flashing notification light or "ding" of an incoming message might mean a new sale, new opportunity, or a customer complaint that needs dealing with. Lori Greiner of Shark Tank once said: "Entrepreneurs are willing to work 80 hours

a week to avoid working 40 hours a week."
It's true. If you are going into business
because you think you will have lots of
spare time, think again.

YOU WILL HAVE CREATIVE CONTROL

Not always the case! Many creatives—
especially designers—decide to work for
themselves so they can pick and choose the
work they do. It doesn't take long to realize
that you will get more work if you take the
jobs that people will pay you for. Over time,
you may be able to take on more creative
work, but if it's a choice between paying the
electricity bill and doing less exciting work,
always take the work.

A potential lack of money, little spare time,
and your creativity resting in the hands of
your clients might make being a creative
entrepreneur sound like a miserable
experience, but it's not all bad. The benefit
is that you can grow at your own pace,
because you get to decide what it is you want
to do—where you want to expand and grow,
and what opportunities to take advantage of.
You will also learn new skills along the way
such as how to code parts of your website,
how to style photos, and how to get more
followers on Instagram. You will learn all
this—and more—not because it is your job,
but because you need to do these things as
well as your job. So yes, it's hard, but it is
worth it.

HOW TO STAY BALANCED, FOCUSED, AND EFFECTIVE

I don't think there is a true balance that you can achieve when you run your own business, but you can certainly try. Balance implies an evenly balanced scale, when in reality it looks more like a seesaw, with each side going up and down every so often—there will always be moments when your family needs your full attention, and other times when your work does.

The best way to stay balanced is to understand that everything is relative. It is not the end of the world if something doesn't go as planned—learn from your mistakes and do better next time.

STAY FOCUSED

Being able to stay focused comes down to keeping your ultimate vision for your company in mind. Don't get distracted from your goals and be single minded in your pursuit of them. If you feel like you are losing focus, remember the bigger picture and your purpose. Why are you doing what you do?

There will be times when your plans or goals change, just be sure that you are not losing sight of what you really want just because of a new idea or because you are distracted by what someone else is doing.

AVOID GETTING OVERWHELMED

Becoming overwhelmed is something that can creep up on us when we least expect it. We say "yes" to a few things here and there and before we know it we are over committed, under resourced, and lack the time to complete everything. As a result, you start feeling stressed and less productive because you are thinking about all the things you should be doing in the future, rather than the one thing you are meant to be doing at that moment.

If you work for yourself, you will probably have to do a lot to keep your business running, whether that's creating your products, providing your services, accounts, marketing, web design, blogging, writing copy, and on and on. You might manage to juggle it all at first, but it can easily get out of control.

It's important to recognize the signs of being overwhelmed and to learn how to overcome it when it strikes. When you start thinking about the long list of tasks you need to get through, you take your focus off the present and into the future. You might start creating to do lists and action plans to try and organize your thoughts, in the hope that you will feel less overwhelmed and more in control. But it won't work—all that planning is taking you away from doing, and no amount of planning will be worth it if you never start the tasks on the list.

So, the next time you feel overwhelmed, just start. Do one thing and focus fully on it. When that is done, do something else. Learn how to refocus on the present. Ask yourself what you can do right now to move your business forward and then take action on it.

DON'T NEGLECT YOURSELF

It is hard for solo entrepreneurs to take a break. You always worry about the emails piling up, the orders you're missing, and the Tweets and Facebook statuses you should be updating.

But you need to take breaks to stay effective. Real breaks. A break where you don't have to worry about emails and where you won't freak out if the Wi-Fi connection isn't working. Everyone benefits from time off every now and again, and even if you're not going away on vacation, taking a break from work can do wonders for your mental health.

HOW TO TAKE A BREAK WHEN YOU WORK FOR YOURSELF

MAKE SURE YOU ARE UP TO DATE WITH ALL CLIENT WORK

Of course, that is a must. If you have regular client work, inform them with plenty of time and make sure they can get hold of you in an emergency (and understand it's only in an emergency!).

PUT A NOTICE UP ON YOUR WEBSITE TO LET CUSTOMERS KNOW ORDERS WILL BE SHIPPED OUT AFTER A CERTAIN DATE

SET AN "OUT OF OFFICE" EMAIL MESSAGE

This is the best way to inform people that it will take longer than normal to reply to their email. It also helps you feel like you are taking a break—the mental shift is important.

TELL PEOPLE ABOUT IT

Tell your friends and family that you are going away or taking a break. Saying it out loud makes it feel real! You can also share this with your social media followers so they know in advance that things will go quiet (and how long for).

TRUST THAT YOUR BUSINESS (OR LIFE) WON'T COME TO AN END IF YOU TAKE LONGER TO REPLY TO EMAILS THAN NORMAL

How many emails do you get per day that are critically important? Probably only a handful. As you have let people know you won't be around and when you are coming back, they will understand.

HOW TO GET THINGS DONE

9

As your business grows, you need to get stricter about using your time more productively. By focusing on the task at hand and being present in what you are doing you'll find it takes less time to complete your to do list. However, if a lack of focus and an overabundance of ideas is sabotaging your attempts to reach your business goals, a few changes to how you work will get you back on track.

CHECK YOUR EMAIL NO MORE THAN THREE TIMES A DAY

If you check your email less, you will get more real work done. Replying to emails all day means you are constantly reacting to what needs to be done rather than taking a proactive approach to getting things done. Be strict with yourself if you need to, and cut down on email checking. Checking your email three times a day—for example, at 9am, 2pm, and 6pm—will allow you to focus on the tasks you need to complete.

You can use project management apps, such as Basecamp and Asana, to stay in touch with current clients. This eliminates much of the back-and-forth emailing involved in longer term projects, as you can just message and upload files within the app. Also, turn off email notifications on your phone—it's hard to focus when you can see a flashing light out of the corner of your eye telling you that you have new messages.

LIMIT SOCIAL MEDIA TO THREE TIMES A DAY

Social media can be one of the biggest time sucks for creative business owners. You want to promote your stuff and connect with other business owners and potential customers, but if you're not careful you can find yourself spending hours on social media every day. Those are hours you'll never get back. Switch it off for a while and you'll get more done.

It's hard to limit social media because it is so easy to use it to fill in dead time, like when you're waiting for the kettle to boil or sitting on the bus. However, too much social media can be draining—limiting your time on it can help you stay more efficient when working. Allocate set times, a few times a day, to check in for a specific period of time.

CLOSE TABS

Have you ever had ten or more tabs open in your web browser at one time? It's easy to do. Maybe you are waiting for a page to load, so you open up a news site to see what's happening. Then you see a few articles you want to read so you open them all up in a different tab. Or maybe you are researching a project so you open up 20 different websites to check different things.

You might think you are being more productive if you are working on multiple things at once, but closing all the extra tabs allows you to focus on the task at hand, thereby completing it quicker. So go ahead, close down your inbox, Facebook, and Twitter, and try working on just the one thing you are supposed to be doing!

SIMPLIFY BUSINESS SYSTEMS

In order to reach your goals for your business you need to set up business systems that allow for growth. This might mean documenting the steps of every process you undertake from client intake, through project workflow, to packaging systems. Systems help you become more efficient and will help hugely when you take on team members in the future.

LIMIT YOUR TO DO LIST

I get it, you're busy and there is never enough time to get everything done, so your to do list is a mile long, or at least doesn't fit on one page. It's awesome you have a ton of ideas and lots of work to do, but it can actually be detrimental to have too many things on your to do list. Get everything out of your brain in a "brain dump list" then put it to one side and concentrate on a daily to do list with essential, prioritized tasks only. Limit your daily list so you don't get overwhelmed and can focus on what needs to get done today.

WORK IN BULK

Group similar tasks together, such as answering emails or promoting your business, and spend a certain amount of time on each. It's more effective to do similar tasks at the same time, rather than going back and forth between them.

Answering emails as you get them can also mean you end up spending every moment in your inbox, as there will always be another one to respond to. Instead, reply to as many as you can within a certain time frame, as this is a better and more effective use of your time. The same technique can be used when you are creating products—making ten of the same necklace at once will be more productive than making them one at a time.

TAKE BREAKS

Constantly working can seem like you are being productive, but you need to take breaks in order for your mind to rest and for your body to recuperate. If you are sitting at your computer, sewing machine, or desk for hours on end you need to start including breaks into your schedule. Not only will it be better for your back but it will give you time to stretch, gather your thoughts, breathe in your surroundings, or just be in the moment.

Try setting a timer to remind yourself to get up from your desk every hour. Then stretch out your legs, brew a cup of tea, and give your eyes a break from what you were doing.

WHEN TO LET GO OF UNACHIEVABLE PERFECTION

You might be thinking, "there's nothing wrong with being a perfectionist," but the problem comes when it gets in the way of you moving forward with your business. Your aim should always be to do things to the best of your ability, but perfection is hardly ever achievable. If you try to get everything perfect before you launch your business you are never going to start. Working on tasks until you get them "just right" sounds good until it takes you double the time it should have. Perfectionist tendencies can have a larger impact on your life by stopping you achieving your potential.

You know if perfectionism is stopping you from achieving great things if:

- You decide you'd rather not do something because you are unsure what to expect or you can't prepare yourself for it.
- You find yourself aiming small so you aren't disappointed.
- You avoid failure by staying within your comfort zone.
- You adopt an "all or nothing" approach: if you can't put 110% into something then you don't do it at all.

It's hard to get started when you know you won't be satisfied with anything less than perfect, especially when you know that perfect isn't really possible. You might be afraid you won't be able to meet expectations, or fulfill the idea you have in your head of the perfect business, the perfect work, and the perfect life. So, you carry on undervaluing yourself and playing small.

PERFECTION PARALYSIS

When perfectionism stops you from trying new things because "it won't be perfect," I call it "perfection paralysis"—it is literally a method of stopping you achieving. If you feel yourself avoiding new things and keeping your goals small, stop telling yourself you can't do it—just try your best and see how it goes. Stop limiting yourself!

When the old habit and feelings of not being good enough resurface, "done is better than perfect" is a good mantra to help you get moving on your goals. It's not about rushing or doing things in a haphazard way—you still need to do your best work and put the best effort you can into each task—but when you get to a point where you are under an unnatural self-imposed pressure, it can be timely to remember. More often than not, your getting it done will still be ten times as good as the next person's, but if you never allow yourself to release it to the world no one will know that.

A simple tip is to focus on progress rather than perfection. One step forward is better than no steps at all, and even if those steps taken aren't perfect, you'll still be closer to your goal than if you didn't even start.

So, if you want to tidy your workspace, don't feel down that you won't ever make it perfect or Pinterest worthy—tidy away one thing or maybe clear your desk. While it won't make your space perfect, you'll be closer than if you left it the way it was. Have your bigger picture in mind for a project, but then break it down into smaller tasks. Focus on one task at a time and make finishing that task the goal. Before long you will have reached your target.

"DONE is better than PERFECT."

SCOTT ALLEN

For example, if you want to start a blog, just start. Buy the domain, set up the hosting, but most of all start writing. Rather than waiting for everything to be perfect, just get started. You can tweak things later—for now, focus on getting it done.

We have one life. Instead of sitting back or limiting our dreams we need to grab them with both hands while we have the chance and be the best we can be. If you want to play big, stop playing small. Stop telling yourself you will be happy with the minimum if it's not true. Give yourself permission to fail and see how far you will go without holding yourself back. There is no shame in wanting more, but in order to get it you have to start. Take one step at a time and don't let the fear of not being perfect put you off achieving something that will not only make you happy, but might even end up changing the world.

FACING FEARS

FEAR. It is one of the main things holding people back from creating the life and business that they deserve. Fear is like a roadblock that looks impossible to pass but with the right strategies you can find your way over.

So what do you fear? Deep down, what is holding you back? Don't overthink it—what's the first thing that comes in your head when you're asked:

*I fear*_____
*because*_____.

Have you ever told yourself you can't do something? Maybe you think you don't have enough time, money, resources, or talent? Well, stop thinking of these things as problems and instead consider them challenges. It's up to you to find a solution and to overcome them creatively.

The dictionary defines fear as "*an unpleasant emotion caused by the belief that someone or something is dangerous, likely to cause pain, or a threat.*"

The key thing there is fear is an emotion. It's not fact. When you fear something, it is not guaranteed to happen, which means you get to decide how you conquer it. In order for you to grow your business you need to have self-worth, value your talents and abilities, and absolutely know who you are so you can be authentic and commit to taking action to create the life you desire. Fear can be overwhelming at first, but by releasing yourself from the power it has over you, you will be able to move forward.

LOOK AT YOUR FEARS FROM A DIFFERENT PERSPECTIVE

Even if the worst happens you can still learn from it—it's OK to fail! Many successful people fail multiple times before accomplishing something great. Some continue to fail, again and again. While it can

be disheartening, failure does not control you, and it should not control your actions. Don't let your fears decide your future.

THINK POSITIVE

When we are fearful it means we don't have the self-belief that we can achieve something.

If you think you're going to fail, then you probably will. You will have already decided that you are not going to make it. Thinking about things in a positive way tells your heart and mind that you believe you can do it. When you believe in yourself you can achieve much more than you ever imagined.

Take running a marathon. If you start the race thinking you aren't going to finish, you probably won't. But if you tell yourself "I can do this," and imagine yourself crossing the finishing line every time your fear starts to surface, you are giving yourself a much greater chance of success.

ACT ON YOUR FEARS

Fear exists to make us question our decisions. We are human, and it's normal to have fears. Instead of trying to ignore them, and letting them fester and grow within you, you need to feel the fear; acknowledge it, listen to it, and then act on it.

Every challenge and every obstacle is an opportunity to learn and to grow, and it's fine to be afraid. But it's not OK to stop striving for things because of that fear. If you do, you'll always be wondering what could have happened had you given it your all. More than anything, you deserve to see what you are capable of.

SETTING BOUNDARIES

Setting boundaries could save your life. Seriously. It's become cool to be a busy, overworked, stressed out, in-demand, coffee-drinking entrepreneur. But why? Are we so worried about looking like we're not working that we overcompensate by taking on too much when the work does arrive? Is that why we're always talking about it? Why are we wearing our busy-ness like a badge of honor? I don't know. What I do know is that we need to put our health and what matters first. Working more doesn't mean you are working hard.

Does this sound like you?

- You check your emails, Tweets, Instagram mentions, Facebook mentions and every other social media mention constantly, throughout the day because you don't want to miss anything?
- You email clients and customers back immediately after receiving an email because you don't want them to think you don't care about them?
- You don't have set office hours or working hours and you find that the line between your work and rest time is starting to blur into one?
- You find it hard to focus on family and relationships because you're always thinking about work, talking about work, or checking up on social media that you hope will bring you more work?
- You work late into the night to try and catch up on everything you need to do?
- You get sick a lot and have no idea why?

If this does sound like you, then you need to set boundaries, and you can help yourself avoid reaching breaking point with the following tips:

SET EMAIL BOUNDARIES

It is easy to reply to emails as soon as they come through, either because you're always online or able to respond from your phone. It might seem like a great idea to answer all emails straight away—it's great customer service, right? Well, yes and no. The problem is, your clients and customers will start to expect immediate replies all the time. If you don't set email boundaries, there will come a time when a client is livid that you've taken three hours to reply to a non-urgent email, rather than giving them the immediate reply they have come to assume. They won't care that you were in a meeting during that time, or you were with another client—it won't cross their minds because you've encouraged them to expect that level of service.

To avoid this, set a limit to the number of times you check your email per day and respond to what you can during the time you allocate. Let your clients know that you will only be answering emails a few times a day so you can do better work and provide them with a better service.

You might also want to use Boomerang for Gmail to schedule emails to send during the office hours of the person receiving it. This helps you communicate with international clients and customers more effectively, while still maintaining boundaries.

SET SOCIAL MEDIA BOUNDARIES

Switch off social media. Immerse yourself fully in your work and when it's done go out and do something unrelated to your work. Social media sucks us in. It is very useful for interacting and engaging with others, but don't let yourself get caught up in constantly checking what everyone else is doing. While you are sitting consumed by what others are doing online, your life is passing you by. Limit your time on social media to short bursts a few times a day. Your followers won't mind, especially if you have high-quality updates—quality over quantity, after all.

SET LIFE AND WORK BOUNDARIES

Work is work. Life is life. Decide what your boundaries will be and when it's OK for them to overlap. If you have children, you might decide that when you are with them, you want to focus on being fully present. When you are on vacation, enjoy it with your family and don't think about work—at all. Plan ahead and arrange your schedule so that it's lighter when you need to go away. Limiting the amount you work on weekends can also help you be healthier and more creative. Go out and get inspired!

GLOSSARY

BLOG

A regularly updated website or web page, typically one run by an individual or small group, that is written in an informal or conversational style.

BRAND EXPERIENCE

A branded customer experience that describes the total impression a potential consumer has and experiences with a company.

BRAND IDENTITY

The visible elements of a brand (such as colors, design, logotype, name, symbol) that together identify and distinguish the brand in the consumers' mind.

BRAND POSITION

Your brand position is where your brand sits in the marketplace in relation to your competitors.

BUSINESS MODEL

A way of designing and planning the successful operation of a business including identifying revenue sources, potential customers, products, and details of financing.

BUSINESS PLAN

A written document that describes how a business is going to achieve its goals. It includes how you will market your business, make money, and operate.

BUSINESS STRATEGY

The means by which a business sets out to achieve its goals and objectives; also known as long-term business planning.

COMPANY CULTURE

The personality of a company that gives an indication of what a company is like to work for.

COMPETITION

The other companies your target customers are able to choose from when they want to buy your product or service.

CONTENT

The text and images that are encountered as part of the user experience on websites.

CONTENT MANAGEMENT SYSTEM

A content management system (CMS) is a computer application that allows publishing, editing and modifying content, organizing, deleting as well as maintenance from a central interface.

CONTENT MARKETING

A method of marketing by providing content in the form of articles or images that have value for your target customer.

CONTENT STRATEGY

The planning, development, and management of content that will be used in your marketing efforts.

CORE VALUES

Core values are the guiding principles that dictate the behavior and actions of a business or person.

COWORKING

Coworking is a new way for independent professionals to work in a shared, collaborative space.

CREATIVE ENTREPRENEUR

Somebody who starts a business using their creative talents.

DOMAIN NAME

The internet address for a business or person online.

ECOMMERCE

The buying and selling of goods and services conducted electronically on the internet.

ELEVATOR PITCH

A short, succinct, and persuasive summary of your company, what you offer, and why the person listening should care.

FOCUS GROUPS

A group of people assembled to participate in a guided discussion about a particular product before it is launched for feedback purposes.

HUMAN RESOURCES

The department of a business or organization that deals with the hiring, administration, and training of personnel.

INFLUENCERS

Individuals who have the power to affect purchase decisions of others because of their (real or perceived) authority, knowledge, and position.

KEYWORDS

Keywords are words or phrases that describe your products, service and web content.

LEAD TIME

Lead time is the time between the start and completion of a production process in publications and products.

MARKET POTENTIAL

The estimated potential sales opportunity of a product or service.

MARKETING PLAN

A comprehensive blueprint that outlines a company's overall marketing efforts.

MARKETING STRATEGY

Your marketing strategy defines how you will raise the visibility of your company with the view to increasing sales and gaining an advantage over your competition.

MARKETPLACE

An online marketplace is an e-commerce website where the products or services are provided by multiple third parties, with the transactions being processed by the marketplace operator.

MISSION STATEMENT

A written statement of the purpose of a company; its reason for existing, its core purpose, and focus, which normally remains unchanged over time.

OPERATIONS

The tasks and functions that enable a business to run smoothly.

PERSONAL BRAND

Personal branding is the process of creating a recognizable professional name and reputation for yourself or your company/business.

POSITIONING STATEMENT

A statement that confirms where you wish your brand to sit in the marketplace.

PRESS KIT

A package of promotional materials provided to the press to brief them about a specific product, service, or company.

PROFITS

The money your business makes after all expenses, salaries, and taxes are accounted for.

SEARCH ENGINE OPTIMIZATION

Search engine optimization (SEO) is the process of increasing the visibility of a website in a search engine's organic search results.

SUSTAINABLE BUSINESS

A business that can be maintained in the long term at a certain rate or level. It can also be used to describe a green, environmentally friendly business.

TARGET MARKET

A target market is a group of potential customers towards which a business has decided to aim its marketing efforts, in order to sell more products or services.

TURNOVER

The amount of money taken by a business in a particular period before expenses or taxes are taken into consideration.

UNIQUE SELLING POINT

The unique selling point (also known as USP) is the thing that differentiates a business from its competitors.

WEB HOSTING

A service providing storage space allowing individuals and organizations to make their website accessible via the World Wide Web.

WHOLESALE

The sale of merchandise to retailers rather than directly to the public.

INDEX

ACKNOWLEDGMENTS

I would like to thank the following people for
all their hard work, advice, and support:

The whole team at Ilex Press and Octopus
Publishing, especially my editor, Natalia
Price-Cabrera, Zara Larcombe, and Julie Weir.

To my darling husband, my mother, Maria,
and my sisters, Melissa and Daniela—thank
you for supporting me in everything that I do.

To my dear children, Joseph and Lily—
Mummy loves you so much, thank you for
inspiring me to do my best every day.

Finally, thank you to the creative
entrepreneurs who were generous with their
time and shared their stories of starting and
growing their businesses, especially Karen
Arthur, Cody Bauchman, Heidi Bowman, Lucy
Edmonds, Sophie Howarth, Vanessa Laven,
Marie Maglaque, Nikki McWilliams, Gabrielle
Treanor, and Nesha Woolery.